THE WONDERS OF THE WORLD
THE WORLD
AND THEIR SECRETS

Questions & Answers

THE WONDERS OF THE WORLD AND THEIR SECRETS

PATRICK RESTELLINI

Larousse & Co., Inc., New York

© 1985 by Libraire Larousse USA Inc.

First published in the United States and Canada by
Larousse & Co., Inc.,
572 Fifth Avenue, New York, N.Y. 10036

ISBN 0-88332-469-5

Printed and bound in Portugal by Resopal

Contents

Introduction

The 'Wonders of the World' was the name given by the ancients to the most beautiful works of art in architecture and sculpture. There were seven of them in antiquity. They were: the Great Pyramid in Egypt; the Hanging Gardens of Semiramis in Babylon; the Mausoleum at Halicarnassus; the statue of Zeus at Olympia; the lighthouse at Alexandria; the Colossus of Rhodes; and the Temple of Artemis at Ephesus.

Six of these wonders have now disappeared, but the ancients left us so many descriptions that we are able to reconstruct drawings of them. Incredibly, the seventh, the most spectacular and the most extraordinary of the seven wonders of the world, still exists today. The Great Pyramid, which is more than 4,000 years old, has survived the centuries without being destroyed by time or the human race.

Since the Great Pyramid many other wonderful structures have been built by the human race, from antiquity to the present day. These monuments often have a secret, either because that was their intention, or because their origins are unknown. Questions are raised which we are sometimes unable to answer fully. This, therefore, gives us the opportunity to speculate as to the origins and purposes of these mysterious monuments.

Of course, this book cannot include all the wonders of our world. There are too many of them! But come with us on a trip through time and space, at the command of civilizations and gods, from the Pyramid of Cheops to the Sydney Opera House, and you will see that throughout the centuries the great structures built by the human race were always worthy of our admiration, whatever their style or period.

How was the Great Pyramid built?

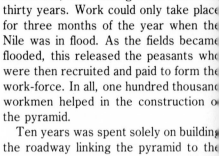

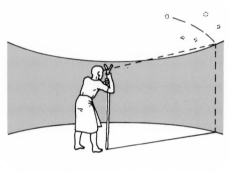

A priest works out the position of the pyramid before it is built. First of all, a wall is built in the centre of the site.

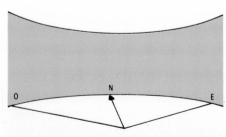

He then marks where the first star appears in the east, and draws a line on the ground. He watches the star until it disappears in the west, and draws a second line. The third line, drawn half-way between the other two, indicates north.

Of the Seven Wonders of the World described by the ancients, the Great Pyramid is the only one which still exists today. It was built in Egypt nearly forty-five centuries ago by the Pharoah Cheops. It stands with the pyramids of Chephren and Mycerinus (the successors of Cheops) on a plateau overlooking the Nile valley, about 9½ miles (15 km) south-west of Cairo. The mysterious Sphinx keeps guard over these gigantic royal tombs.

The pyramid of Cheops forms the main part of this burial complex. Its size is impressive: 137 m (450 ft) high: 230 sq m (825 sq ft), covering a ground area of 5 hectares (12½ acres)! 2,300,000 blocks of stone had to be cut, each stone weighing 2 to 3 tonne (approximately 2 to 3 ton).

The four sides of the pyramid, inclined at an angle of 51°52′, are positioned very accurately to face the four points of the compass. The architects were able to do this with such great precision due to the extremely accurate astronomical observations made by Egyptian scholars.

The entrance to the pyramid is situated 18 m (59 ft) above ground-level on the north side. A complex network of descending and ascending galleries lead to the centre of the pyramid, where three funeral chambers have been built, each leading in to the next. This strange arrangement was the result of changes made to the original plan during construction of the pyramid.

According to the Greek historian Herodotus, the building work lasted for thirty years. Work could only take place for three months of the year when the Nile was in flood. As the fields became flooded, this released the peasants who were then recruited and paid to form the work-force. In all, one hundred thousand workmen helped in the construction of the pyramid.

Ten years was spent solely on building the roadway linking the pyramid to the river, which was used for transporting materials. The stone blocks were quarried from the broad limestone banks of the Nile and were transported along the river by boat. They were smoothed off on site, before being assembled.

As the pyramid grew, the stones were hauled on sledges up ramps. The ramps were made of sun-dried bricks, and gravel and mud extracted from the river. They were then strengthened with poles, to reduce the wear from the runners of the sledge.

Once it was built, the pyramid was covered in smooth limestone, starting at the top, and the ramps were gradually dismantled.

A funeral temple and five pits were built at the foot of the pyramid. Inside the pits, cedar wood boats, 30 to 40 m (98 to 131 ft) long, were found still intact. These boats had been specially built for the Pharaoh's voyage into the next world.

The Great Pyramid of Cheops was completed about 2600 BC, but it probably never held the body of the Pharaoh. The sarcophagus, which was to have contained the embalmed body, remained empty, and the heavy granite grilles, which were intended to seal the tomb, were never placed in position. Nevertheless, this monument, with its spectacular size and the number of complicated calculations required to build it, is a major example of engineering in ancient Egypt.

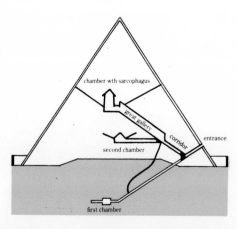

chamber with sarcophagus

great gallery

second chamber

corridor

entrance

first chamber

Left: cross-section of the Great Pyramid showing the descending and ascending galleries leading to the three funeral chambers.

8

The Great Pyramid, floodlit. The tombs of
high dignitaries can be seen in the foreground.

The pyramid of the King Zoser, at Saqqara
(third dynasty, 2613 BC), is a *mastaba* or
stepped pyramid. The steps were supposed to
enable the soul of the dead person to ascend to
heaven. During the fourth dynasty, the
Pharaoh Sneferu built royal tombs without
steps: these are the 'true' pyramids.

Thanks to an ingenious hydraulic system, and to a very large number of slaves, the gardens of Babylon flowered throughout the year. They formed a splendid artificial oasis in the middle of the desert.

How were the Hanging Gardens of Semiramis created in the open desert?

According to Persian legends, the Hanging Gardens of Babylon were named after Princess Semiramis, who ruled over the Assyrian Empire at the end of the ninth century BC. In fact, they were built in the reign of Nebuchadnezzar II, King of Babylon, two centuries later.

It was because of the King's love for his wife, Amyitis, that he had these gardens built. He wanted to remind her of the trees and flowers of her native country, Persia.

The gardens rose above the city walls, and resembled a green hillside with several levels. Terraces and shady walks were laid out on each level, and these were decorated with native or exotic flowers. The water supply was provided by an ingenious system of buckets attached to a chain. The chain turned continuously, bringing water from the river to the upper levels. The water then fell in cascades from level to level. In this way, the gardens bloomed throughout the year.

The Greek historian, Herodotus, tells how people came from all quarters to admire the wonder of these beautiful gardens. Babylon stood in the open desert on the banks of the Euphrates, about 62 miles (100 km) south of what is now Baghdad (in Iraq). Imagine, then, the extraordinary sight this tiny island of lush vegetation provided when travellers approached the town. Indeed, the armies of Alexander the Great were most impressed by the gardens when they entered the city in 331 BC.

Why did Erostratus destroy the Temple at Ephesus?

The city of Ephesus was founded by the Ionians during the great migrations of the Greeks in Asia Minor around 1000 BC. It flourished rapidly as a result of its trading activities. At that time, it was also the centre for the worship of Artemis, the great Goddess of Fertility, who had been honoured for thousands of years in Anatolia. (Do not confuse her with the classical Greek goddess, Artemis, the cold maiden huntress, sister of Apollo.)

A little before the middle of the sixth century BC, the inhabitants of Ephesus started to build a temple worthy of their goddess and of their affluent city. They called upon the architects Theodorus of Samos and Chersiphon and Metagenes of Crete to take charge of the building work.

The King of Lydia, the wealthy Croesus (561–541 BC) insisted on helping with the decoration of the building, and offered several columns to the temple. According to Pliny the Younger, the building was completed in 550 BC and measured 115×55 m (377×181 ft). It contained 127 marble columns, each 19 m (62 ft) high. More than one third of these columns were decorated with wonderful reliefs.

Legend has it that in 356 BC, on the very night that Alexander the Great was born, an inhabitant of the city, who was called Erostratus, set fire to the temple, completely destroying it. He did this to ensure that his name would always be remembered.

A new temple was built on the same site. It was set on a platform reached by a broad staircase with fourteen steps. The ancients, who were entranced by the splendour of the building, classed it among the Wonders of the World. Its richness and radiance were so great that it attracted crowds of pilgrims, from all over Greece and Asia Minor, to honour the goddess.

In the first century AD, the Roman Emperor Nero took possession of the stupendous riches which had accumulated in the temple. In AD 263 the Temple of Artemis was pillaged by the Goths, but it was restored yet again. However, the appearance of Christianity pushed it into insignificance. Deserted and abandoned, it was used as a stone-pit by the builders of the Saint Sophia basilica in Constantinople.

The temple at Ephesus reflected the splendour of the city in the sixth century BC. It is dedicated to Artemis, the Goddess of Fertility, who is often confused with the Roman goddess Diana.

IUPITER
OLYMPICU

Why was the Zeus of Olympia the most beautiful statue of antiquity?

The statue of Zeus, erected at Olympia by the wealthy citizens of Elis, was the work of the great Phidias, the best sculptor of the Golden Age of ancient Greece.

The city of Elis guarded the sanctuary of Olympia in the Peloponnese, in Greece. In the fifth century BC, the inhabitants of the city decided to construct a temple to the glory of Zeus.

In order to provide the building with a statue worthy of the master of the gods and of men, the city commissioned the most celebrated sculptor of the time, the Athenian Phidias (490–431 BC). He was assisted in his task by the painter Paranios and the engraver Colotes. The statue, which was about 12 m (39 ft) tall, showed Zeus sitting on his throne. In his out-stretched right hand, he held a statue made of gold and ivory which symbolized

Victory, and in his left hand he held a large sceptre surmounted by an eagle. A cloak fell from one shoulder to cover the thighs and legs of the god. The naked parts, the head, torso and feet, were of painted ivory: the cloak, the bust and the hair were encrusted with precious stones. The ebony and bronze throne was decorated with ivory and gold panels, precious stones and paintings.

Unfortunately, nothing remains of this work of art, which was so admired by the ancients. It was taken to Constantinople at the beginning of the fifth century AD, by the Roman Emperor Theodosus II, and was destroyed by fire in 475.

12

What still remains of the Mausoleum at Halicarnassus?

In the fourth century BC, the Persian Empire was made up of *satrapies,* or provinces. One of these was called Caria, an independent kingdom under Greek influence. Mausoleus, the *satrap* (governor) of Caria, took advantage of its remoteness from the chief Persian towns, and soon started to act as a true king. He began to transform his province, using Greek cities as his model.

He built a new capital beside the sea, at Halicarnassus. He provided it with magnificent buildings decorated by famous Greek artists, whom he invited to his court.

He erected a magnificent marble tomb, which was completed on his death by his wife–sister, Artemis. This building became known as a 'Mausoleum'. Two architects and four Greek sculptors helped in the construction. With an overall height of 42 m (138 ft), this massive monument was erected on a tall base, surrounded by Ionic columns. A 24° pyramid, topped by a statue showing a triumphal chariot driven by Mausoleus, crowned the whole edifice. Friezes were sculpted on the four sides of the Mausoleum and showed the Greeks fighting the Centaurs and the Amazons, and a chariot race.

The building was still standing until the eleventh century AD, when it was demolished by the Knights of St John, to provide the materials required to build a stronghold at Halicarnassus.

The only items still in existence are some carved fragments which were found during excavations. These are now preserved in the British Museum, London.

The fame of the great burial monument erected to Mausoleus by his wife has passed down through the centuries: the word 'mausoleum' is still used today to refer to the tomb of a great person.

What was the method used to light the lighthouse at Alexandria?

Of the Seven Wonders of the World, the lighthouse at Alexandria is the only monument which was built for a practical purpose: to help shipping in the Mediterranean Sea. The lighthouse was erected at the eastern end of the island of Pharos, in the Nile delta, to mark the entrance to the port of Alexandria. Alexandria (founded by Alexander the Great after his conquest of Egypt) was one of the great centres of the ancient world.

The lighthouse was built in an octagonal shape, three stories high, at the beginning of the third century BC. It was reputedly 110 m (361 ft) high. The top was decorated with bronze tritons, and the statue of a god 7 m (23 ft) tall. The god brandished a lighted torch, which was reflected by convex mirrors into the distance, for over 3 miles (5 km)! A system of lifting devices raised the fuel (which was probably wood, but may also have been oil or pitch) to the top of the lighthouse.

The lighthouse took the name of the island, and that is why the name 'pharos' has become a word for a lighthouse and is now used to describe any tower used to guide shipping.

Unfortunately, nothing remains of thi[s] magnificent creation of antiquity, as it wa[s] destroyed in the fourteenth century by [a] violent earthquake. However, thi[s] monument was greatly admired by th[e] ancients, and they have left us sever[al] drawings of it.

The lighthouse at Alexandria was built in the reign of King Ptolemy Philadelphus of Egypt (309–246 BC), who was a descendant of one of Alexander the Great's lieutenants.

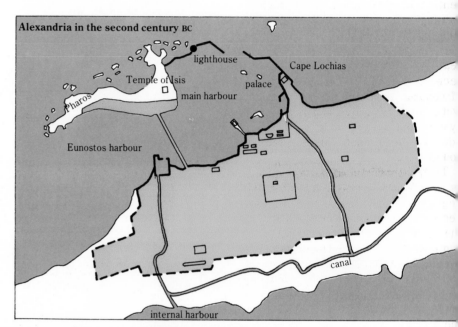

Alexandria in the second century BC

PHAROS

What did the Colossus of Rhodes represent?

By the third century BC, Rhodes had become the centre of a vast trading network in the Mediterranean. It possessed three harbours and enormous warehouses, where wine, oil, corn and exotic produce were stored.

This republic was one of the great centres of distribution in the ancient world. Its merchants understood the importance of being politically neutral and the importance of the freedom of the seas. As a neutral state, it was able to receive ships from Italy, Greece, Macedonia, Asia and Africa. Its banks were particularly active, and its monetary system and navigation laws had been adopted by most Mediterranean countries.

The people of Rhodes grew confident as a result of their prosperity and, at the beginning of the third century BC, they decided to build a huge bronze statue to the god protecting their city — Helios, the sun-god. It would remind them of the victory gained over the Macedonian, Demetrios Poliorcetus, who came to lay siege to the town. The work was entrusted to Chares of Lindos, a pupil of the sculptor Lysippus.

The statue was 33 m (108 ft) high, and showed a very beautiful young man with a crown of golden rays on his head. Tradition has it that the Colossus had one foot on each end of the breakwaters which surrounded the harbour. Without doubt, this is incorrect, because the harbour entrance would have been much too narrow. It is more likely that the statue was intended to stand at the entrance or at the far end of the harbour it was protecting.

The Colossus was destroyed by a violent earthquake in 224 BC, less than a century after it had been erected.

Although, thanks to the generosity of other kingdoms, Rhodes rose rapidly from the ruins and regained its former splendour, the statue, alas, was never rebuilt.

The giant statue of Helios, the Greek sun-god, most probably stood at the far end of the harbour at Rhodes. It was built at the beginning of the third century BC, and was destroyed by an earthquake shortly afterwards.

Has the secret of the cromlech at Stonehenge been revealed?

At the end of the Neolithic period (the polished Stone Age), about 2500 BC, a mysterious circle of stones was built at Stonehenge, in southern England. It is called a cromlech. The name comes from the Breton words 'crom' (curve) and 'lech' (place).

Originally, this monument consisted of about one hundred large stones, or megaliths. About forty of these are still in place, arranged in a circle.

Excavations carried out on the site have shown that Stonehenge was constructed in several phases.

At the beginning of the second millennium BC, a ditch, with an entrance gap to the south-east, marked the boundary of a circle 100 m (328 ft) in diameter. Inside the circle fifty-six pits formed a ring running parallel to the ditch.

The first change came two centuries later when a double circle of stones was erected. These stones had been cut from a blue rock quarried 100 miles (160 km) from the site!

Some years later, at the beginning of the Bronze Age, the lay-out of the monument was changed yet again. Sandstone blocks, 7 m (23 ft) tall and some weighing up to 50 tonne (49 ton), were quarried about 19 miles (30 km) north of Stonehenge. These, along with the old stones, were arranged into four circles. The largest circle was 30 m (98 ft) in diameter. It consisted of thirty monoliths (single stones) more than 4 m (13 ft) tall joined together by lintels. Inside the second circle, five groups of triliths (two supports each 8 m (26 ft) high, topped by a lintel) formed a horseshoe, and a long flat stone was placed in the centre on the ground.

It is generally thought that this monument was a shrine connected with the worship of the sun. In fact, it has been shown that the two horseshoes of Stonehenge are aligned so that, at the summer solstice (21 June), the sun rises along the centre line of the monument, or a menhir (standing stone) in front of the shrine.

A place to worship the sun? An astronomical observatory? The theories are fascinating, but none has been totally convincing. The cromlech of Stonehenge remains a mystery.

Left: the transportation and erection of the enormous stones at Stonehenge must have posed some extraordinary problems for the people of this early period. The most probable methods, illustrated here, are described in the box opposite.

Above: the cromlech as it once must have appeared.

One explanation... but not certain!

It certainly was a remarkable achievement for the Stone Age people to transport these large stones and erect them at Stonehenge. Unfortunately, very little is known of the methods used. However, from their observations, archaeologists have been able to make some suggestions.

Some stones, cut from quarries 200 miles (320 km) away from the site, were probably transported on rafts, and then hauled on sledges, by hundreds of people pulling ropes.

The erection of the stone was the most difficult part. It is thought that a trench was hollowed out and strengthened on three sides. The monolith was then slipped into the hole and pulled into an upright position with ropes. The lintel was raised a centimetre at a time, through the use of wedges, poles and then platforms. This procedure continued until the platform reached the top of the stone pillars, when the lintel could be levered into place across the upright stones.

17

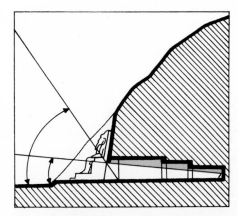

In the Nile valley, the large artificial lake, which formed after the construction of the Aswan dam, has covered many historical treasures.

How were the temples of Abu Simbel moved?

On the left bank of the Nile, north of the second cataract, stand the temples of Abu Simbel, hollowed out of the rock. These ancient Egyptian monuments were built by Rameses II, around 1360 BC, and were dedicated to himself. To the left stands the temple of the Pharaoh with four huge seated statues (colossi). They are 20 m (66 ft) tall and are of the king himself. A smaller temple dedicated to his wife, Queen Nefertiti, stands 100 m (328 ft) to the right.

In Rameses' temple, two chambers, decorated with paintings showing the fighting prowess and magnificence of Rameses, lead to the shrine situated 63 m (207 ft) beneath the mountainside. There the Pharaoh, in the form of a statue, sits among the gods. Twice a year, in mid-February and mid-October, the first ray of the rising sun falls on to the back of this chamber, lighting up the sacred statues and bringing the Pharaoh out of the shadows. This alignment was calculated to one-tenth of a degree.

The temples of Abu Simbel, however, no longer occupy their original positions. They have been reconstructed on a platform built 60 m (197 ft) higher up.

Why was this enormous task undertaken? To save the temples from being submerged by Lake Nasser, the artificial lake created by the Aswan Dam.

How did they set about it? A special dam, 25 m (82 ft) high and 360 m (1,181 ft) long, was constructed between the temples and the river, to protect the site from the rising waters. Pumping stations were installed to avoid any seepage.

The first phase of the work consisted of removing the whole mass of rock situated above the temples. An enormous embankment of sand covered the entire rock-face to protect the statues, and scaffolding was erected inside the chambers to support the walls and ceilings. The rock above could then be dug out to within 80 cm (31 in) of the temples' ceilings. About 300,000 tonne (295,200 ton) of material were taken away.

Once this work had been completed, the temples were cut up into blocks weighing between 20 and 30 tonne (approximately 20 to 30 ton). Giant cranes lifted the blocks on to trucks with special platforms. The trucks then ran along a road constructed on top of the embankment.

Finally, the temples were rebuilt on the new site, without any alteration to their alignment or surroundings. The rock-face and the ceilings of the inner chambers were strengthened with an invisible layer of reinforced concrete. A concrete dome was constructed above this, to support the covering of rock which formed the original hillside.

Opposite: close-up of one of the four giant heads of Rameses II, at the entrance to the temple at Abu Simbel.

Above: height of the sun above the horizon. The small curve shows the sun lighting up the back of the temple to an angle of 4°: this occurs only twice a year, in mid-February and mid-October. The large curve shows that at a greater angle, the sun does not go beyond the entrance (Unesco document).

Above and right: the thick black line indicates the concrete reinforcements which support the weight of the artificial hill.

Cross-section of the Temple of Rameses II

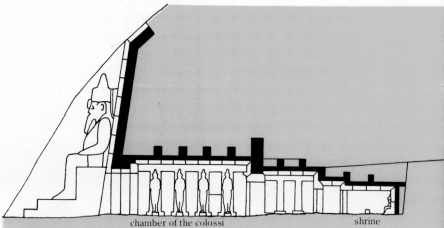

chamber of the colossi   shrine

Above: the temples of Abu Simbel rebuilt on their new site, safe from the waters. In the foreground you can see the temple of Queen Nefertiti.

Below: the entrance to the temple of Rameses II. Beside the legs of the four statues of the King can be seen statues of his wife and sons.

Rescued from the waters of the river Nile, just like Moses!

Upstream of Aswan, many temples of the pharaohs flanked the river Nile; some of them became churches when Christianity was introduced into Nubia.

The construction of the Aswan Dam threatened to destroy these relics of the ancient Egyptians. However, a large-scale international aid enabled twenty-three of these ancient tombs, including the temples of Abu Simbel, to be rescued. Some were dismantled and rebuilt at higher positions, close to their original site; others were moved quite a distance. When the job was completed, four monuments were offered by the Egyptian Government to the countries which had provided a large part of the money to finance this very costly operation.

What remains of the Olmec civilization?

In 1862, a peasant, busy clearing the jungle in the coastal region of eastern Mexico, noticed something lying embedded in the ground. He thought that it was the base of an overturned cooking pot. Imagine his surprise when, as he tried to free the object, centimetre by centimetre, he unearthed an enormous head, more than 2 m (6 ft) tall and weighing several tonnes, sculpted from basalt!

Sixty-three years later, two American archaeologists, while searching for Mayan remains, discovered other heads of the same type. They also discovered a pyramid of beaten earth 35 m (115 ft) high, and several altars and steles carved from basalt. This occurred at La Venta, a small island surrounded by marshes.

Discoveries and excavations in the jungle eventually multiplied. The evidence could not be denied: these inhospitable regions to the south of the Gulf of Mexico at one time must have been the centre of a mysterious civilization. Indeed, the Olmecs are now considered to be the first civilization of Central America.

More than 1000 years BC, these mysterious people erected pyramids and temples, sculpted steles and altars with unparalleled skill, carved stones of jade, and invented hieroglyphic script, before disappearing at the beginning of the Christian era, without anyone knowing the reason why.

We know practically nothing of the history of the Olmecs. Only their art is known to us, through the polished axes, sculptures, jade figurines and steles discovered on numerous sites.

The dozen or so enormous basalt heads which have been found are a further puzzle. These gigantic heads never had a body and were designed to stand on a pedestal. They vary in height from 1.6 m to 3 m (5 ft to 10 ft) and in weight from 15 to 30 tonne (approximately 15 to 30 ton). They all represent human faces with flat noses and thick lips. The head is covered with a kind of cap with side-pieces. Were they created to honour dead chieftains, or were they gods or heroes? We do not know.

Here too, as at Stonehenge or on Easter Island, one is astounded by the amazing effort and ingenuity required to transport these monoliths from the basalt quarries 62 miles (100 km) away, to their present site.

Three sculptures discovered at La Venta, which was one of the three ceremonial centres of the mysterious Olmecs, the oldest civilization in Central America.

Why was Persepolis built?

Lost in the middle of a vast expanse of semi-desert, several slender columns stand on a man-made terrace, 18 m (59 ft) high, cut out of the mountainside. This is all that remains today of Persepolis, city of the Persians and former residence of the Great Kings. It was founded in 518 BC to reflect the power and unity of the Achaemenid Empire, which was then at the peak of its glory.

Persepolis was situated in the Fars. Unlike Susa, it was never a political capital. It was a town solely for festivals and ceremonies. The sovereign, surrounded by his court, went there each spring to receive homage from delegations from the many provinces which formed the immense empire at that time.

These delegations were accommodated in tents on the vast plain facing the terrace. On New Year's Day, they would ascend the 108 steps of the enormous staircases leading to the terrace. The would then pass through a large gateway guarded by huge statues of winged bull with human heads, and enter the grea audience hall. It was 75 sq m (269 sq ft and could easily hold 10,000 people! The numerous bas reliefs, which still decorate the staircases leading to Darius' palace have enabled us to reconstruct the order of ceremonies and the pageantry which accompanied the delegates as they paid homage to the king.

Persepolis continued to add splendou upon splendour. The successors o Darius built the 'Hall of a Hundre Columns', a beautiful palace in which t receive the delegations. Its wealth was s great that the gates were plated with bronze and gold. The statues decorating the palace wore bracelets and necklace of precious stones, and today you can stil see the holes into which they were set

A Mede dignitary, recognizable by his domed head-dress (detail from a frieze).

General view of the Palace of Darius.

The city, however, was never completed. In 330 BC, Alexander the Great seized the city after defeating the Persian army on the borders of Granicus, then at Gaugameles. He burnt down the royal residence after having carefully emptied it of its treasures, which were carried away by 20,000 mules and 5,000 camels.

Plan of the terrace

1 The Great Staircase
2 Xerxes' Gateway
3 Apadana
4 Darius' Palace
5 Xerxes' Palace
6 Central Palace
7 Hall of a Hundred Columns
8 Treasury

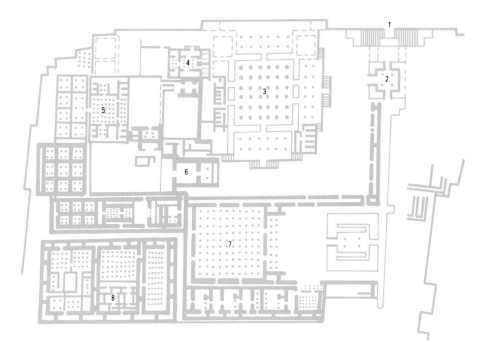

Left: the parade of twenty-three nations (audience hall or Apadana).

Below: vassals bearing offerings (Palace of Xerxes).

What is the largest structure ever built?

No monument has required as much human effort in its construction as the Great Wall of China. It is more than 3,107 miles (5,000 km) long and took two thousand years to build. It used 180 million cu m (235 million cu yd) of earth and 60 million cu m (78 million cu yd) of stone.

It was begun in the fifth century BC, and was completed, after several interruptions, in the sixteenth century, under the Ming dynasty. It runs from east to west, from the Yellow Sea north of Peking to the Gobi Desert, like a stone snake, and it can be seen from the moon. It closely follows the contours of the land, which is particularly rugged in this mountainous region.

Hundreds of thousands of soldiers, peasants and prisoners helped to build it. Many of them died on the job, and some were buried directly in the walls.

The original construction consisted of large embankments of earth and rocks. Under the Ming dynasty, however, dressed stone was used, and only these parts of the wall still remain today.

The wall is 7 m (23 ft) high, 5 m (16 ft) wide at the top and 6 m (20 ft) wide at the bottom. A roadway, protected by battle-ments, was constructed along the top. It was wide enough to allow five horsemen, or ten front line soldiers, or even carts to pass. A system of gutters and drains caught the rain-water and discharged it away from the wall. Two-storey look-out towers were spaced at intervals along the crenelated wall. At certain strategic points, there was a double wall, a triple wall, and even a five-fold wall!

The Great Wall of China was built primarily for defensive reasons. It was designed to protect the northern boundary of the Chinese empire from the *Hu* ('barbarians' in Chinese), who were nomadic, war-like tribes. Permanent troops, composed of soldier-peasants and garrisoned soldiers, were given the task of guarding and maintaining the wall, and repelling any attack. From 166 BC, a clever system of signalling allowed the garrisons to keep in contact with each other (using flags and smoke during the day, and fires at night), and also to give warnings to the Imperial Court within a matter of hours.

The Great Wall also made it possible to transport reinforcements and goods into a region which was not easily accessible.

Above and opposite: of the many fortifications erected by the Chinese against the barbarians from the steppes, only the Great Wall of the Mings (fifteenth to seventeenth century) still remains.

Even if it did not provide effective protection against invasions, some historians say that it encouraged the cultivation of land, by breaking the force of the wind off the steppe.

Some well-preserved sites have been restored, particularly to the north-west of Peking. Today, they are a place for outings, which are much appreciated by the Chinese from the capital and by foreign tourists.

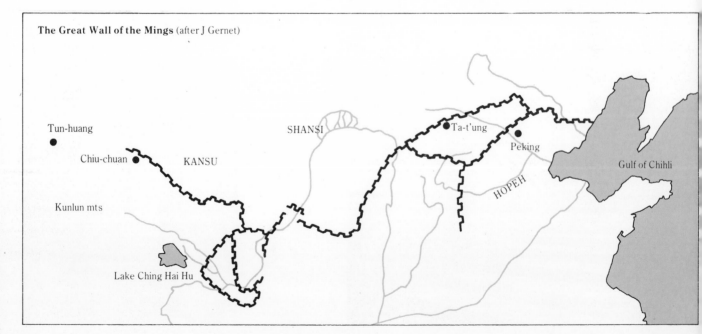

The Great Wall of the Mings (after J Gernet)

Tun-huang

Chiu-chuan   KANSU

Kunlun mts

Lake Ching Hai Hu

SHANSI

Ta-t'ung

Peking

HOPEH

Gulf of Chihli

Why do the columns of the Parthenon lean slightly?

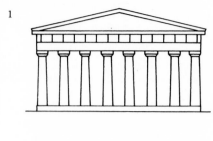

Above: the correction of optical illusions in the construction of the Parthenon.

1 The temple as it appears;
2 As it would appear if it were built with lines which were exactly horizontal or vertical;
3 The way it is actually built.

The Golden Age of Greece saw many wonders. In the middle of the fifth century BC, Pericles, the leader of the democratic party in Athens, decided to erect a vast group of buildings on the Acropolis. The most important of these was to be a temple, the Parthenon, dedicated to Athena, the goddess protecting the city. The Greeks believed Athena had saved them from the Persian invaders by ensuring the victory of Salamis (480 BC).

Pericles appointed Phidias, the greatest sculptor and architect Greece had ever known, to take charge of the construction. He and his successors directed the work, which took forty years to complete. In order to provide the money for this enormous project, Pericles used the profits from the silver mines at Lauron, and the proceeds from the tax imposed on the states under Athens' rule.

The Parthenon is next to perfection. What is the secret? The architects, Ictinos and Callicrates, wanted to achieve perfect balance. They used ingenious methods to correct the optical illusions which would have occurred as a result of the building's great size.

If they had used perfectly horizontal and vertical lines, the building would have appeared to lean outwards and taper towards the base. For this reason, the stylobate is not completely flat. It arches by 11 cm (4 in) at the mid-point of the main façades.

In the same way, the columns tilt

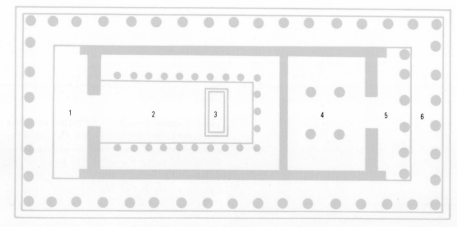

Left: ground plan of the Parthenon.

1 Pronaos
2 Cella
3 Statue of Athena
4 Parthenon
5 Opisthodomos
6 Frieze

The Parthenon seen from the north-east. This monument, consecretated to the goddess Athena, protectress of the city of Athens, is considered to be the model of Doric Greek architecture. It was built with an amazing ingenuity which illustrates the degree of refinement reached by architects in the age of Pericles.

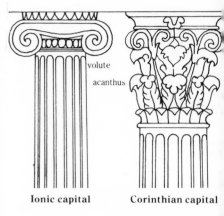

Ionic capital   Corinthian capital

volute
acanthus

Doric order

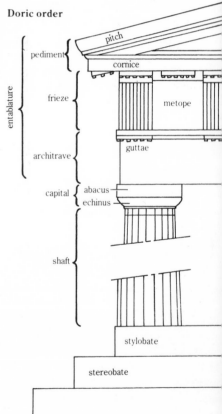

pitch
pediment
cornice
entablature
frieze
metope
architrave
guttae
capital
abacus
echinus
shaft
stylobate
stereobate

slightly inwards, so as not to give the appearance of leaning outwards. The columns are tilted at such an angle, that if they were extended, they would meet 1,500 m (4,923 ft) above ground level. Two-fifths of the way up, the columns have a slightly bulbous shape, so that they do not appear to be thinner in the middle. The four corner columns are thicker and closer together than their neighbours.

The temple is in the Doric style, and is surrounded by a frieze in the Ionic style (the only example of this in Greek architecture). This was the work of Phidias and his pupils.

The Acropolis was a symbol of Athenian grandeur and power, and it followed Athens in its decline. The Parthenon was transformed into a church in the second century, then into a mosque by the Turks in the fifteenth century. This most beautiful of temples was partly destroyed two centuries later by the Venetians, when they attacked the city.

Despite the cruelty of Fate, the Parthenon remains the symbol of freedom and of the love of beauty, which typified Athens in the classical period.

Above: west colonnade of the Parthenon (built 448–432 BC), the jewel of the Acropolis, earthly home of the gods, and a sacred symbol of Greece's omnipotence during this period.

The Acropolis at Athens

Naturally elevated positions, such as rocks, plateaux or hills, offer the best strategic sites for defence. It is not surprising, therefore, that the Athenians transformed the sharp, rocky 150 m (492 ft) high hill overlooking the Attic plain, into a citadel. It became the centre for shrines, temples and the main administrative departments and formed the Acropolis or 'high town' (from the Greek words 'akros' meaning 'raised' and 'polis' meaning 'city'). In the sixth century BC, several buildings were erected in succession. The four principal ones are the Parthenon (447–431 BC), the Propylaea (437–432 BC), the temple of Athena Nike (448–421 BC) and the Erectheion (421–406 BC).

28

What do the giant statues of Nemrut Dag represent?

Five giant heads, 2.5 m to 3 m (8 ft to 10 ft) tall, perch on the summit of Nemrut Dag, 2,150 m (7,056 ft) above sea-level. They lie on the bare ground, and gaze upon the barren mountains of the Anti-Taurus in Turkey.

These are the remains of a monumental tomb erected to Antiochus I (69–34 BC), the King of Commagene, whose kingdom was situated in the region of the Upper Euphrates. Around the beginning of the Christian era Commagene was a small, independent state between Parthia and the Roman Empire. It was rich and prosperous.

Little is known about Antiochus I. His name first appears when he managed to reach an agreement with Pompey in 64 BC which safeguarded the kingdom's boundaries. But in AD 72, the state was taken over by the emperor Vespasian.

It seems that Antiochus, an Eastern prince, received a Greek education. He was descended from Alexander the Great, the Macedonian, on his mother's side, and from Darius, the Persian, on his father's side. This double family link is found on the sculpted bas reliefs decorating his shrine, which was discovered by a Turkish geologist in 1881.

His tomb consists of a burial mound of round pebbles. It is 50 m (164 ft) high and 170 m (558 ft) in diameter at the base. It is bordered to the north, west and east by terraces built on high walls. Stone eagles and lions guarded the approaches to the tomb.

The best preserved of the stone figures at the burial site are five giant statues of seated figures which stand between an eagle and a lion on the terrace. They are 9 m (30 ft) tall. Today the heads of these statues lie at a lower level, perhaps as the result of an earthquake or vandalism. They are representations of King Antiochus, surrounded by gods belonging to the Graeco–Iranian culture.

This shrine has not yet revealed all its secrets. Despite many 'digs', the burial chamber where Antiochus is supposed to rest among his treasures has still not been found. It is hoped, however, that it will soon be discovered by the use of ultra-modern sound equipment.

This massive eagle's head, cut from the sandstone, was a royal symbol.

Below left and right: the giant heads of gods and of King Antiochus I at Nemrut Dag. These remains, defaced and out of position, still keep guard beside the tomb which has not yet revealed its secret.

Has Easter Island revealed its secrets?

Lost in the middle of the Pacific Ocean, 1,988 miles (3,200 km) from the coast of Chile, Easter Island stands with its mysterious giant statues, the 'Moai', whose identity is still unknown.

On Easter Day in 1722, Dutch sailors serving under Admiral Jacob Roggeven, first discovered these stone giants. They were amazed by their strange presence on this barren island, with its thousand or so inhabitants of Polynesian origin.

The statues had been carved from tuff (a soft, volcanic rock). There are about a thousand of them. They are busts of people with long ears, and they vary in size from 3 m to 20 m (9 ft to 66 ft), and in weight between 5 and 40 tonne (approximately 5 and 40 ton)! The largest, weighing 100 tonne (98 ton), has never been erected, and lies unfinished in the island's main quarry, on the side of the volcano Rano-Raraku. Most of the statues are set directly in the ground, although some rest on stone platforms. They have a kind of tall cylinder on their enormous flat heads. Is this a hat or a coil of hair? It is known that the old Pascuans used to put up their long hair like this.

For some strange reason, all these statues, with a few exceptions, are turning their backs on the sea. They are looking, with their mysteriously stern faces, towards the centre of the island. Perhaps the people who carved them arrived on the island after braving a raging sea.

What great mysteries for such a small island! Wherever one goes, a host of questions beset the visitor: what was the purpose of these striking statues, with their thoughtful expressions, broad noses, lipless mouths, and eyes worn away by time? Who do they represent? When, how and why were they erected? There are no definite answers unfortunately, but some fascinating theories have been put forward.

The famous group of seven 'Moai', situated inland. Unlike most of the statues on the island, who stand with their backs to the sea, this group face the ocean.

One theory is that the island is the remains of a submerged continent, where a great civilization once prospered. Another theory, drawing on Polynesian legends and native folklore, maintains that people came from the islands of Oceania to colonize Easter Island towards the end of the first millennium. The story is that two tribes lived on the island: the Long Ears and the Short Ears. The Long Ears were sculptors belonging to a high caste which ruled over the Short Ears. The Short Ears were farmers and they had to do the hardest work; maybe they transported the statues which the Long Ears had carved in the likeness of their ancestors. After a time, the Short Ears revolted. The war between the two tribes lasted for a very long time and ended with the destruction of the Long Ears. This could explain why 160 statues remain unfinished, while others have been

One of the mysterious statues found on Easter Island. Is it an idol or a deified ancestor of the ancient Pascuans?

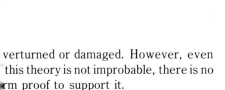

verturned or damaged. However, even this theory is not improbable, there is no rm proof to support it.

The statues are not the only puzzle. At he top of the volcano Rano-Kau, facing he sea, pictures have been carved on undreds of basalt rocks. They mainly how the 'bird-man', and are evidence of a ult which died out in the last century.

What a mystery Easter Island is! Where did its first inhabitants come from? When will someone succeed in decoding he mysterious writing engraved on the ablets? Why were the eyes of the statues o important, and—as we now now—so delicately carved after the tatues had been put in place?

On Easter Island, questions arise with early every step. It is a fascinating won-er of the world, whose stone giants have ept guard over its secrets for centuries.

This petroglyph (stone carving), depicting the 'bird-man', is evidence of a cult which originated on the island at the end of the seventeenth century, and which died out in the last century.

What we know... and what we don't know

It has been possible to reconstruct the way in which the statues of Easter Island were made.

Great quantities of chisels made of basalt (toki), which were used by the stone-cutters, have been found on old work sites. Two methods of working the stone were used. The first was to detach a block of stone, and then sculpt it. The second was to sculpt the statue directly into the rock until finally it was attached only by a rib at the back. Once the sculpture had been released, it was set up in a large hole, and the back was smoothed off.

When this operation had been completed, the large stone was transported to its final resting place, sometimes a distance of 9 miles (15 km) or so.

How were these giants moved, handled and erected on ground which was, in addition, hilly? Unfortunately no one has been able to give an acceptable explanation. It is thought that large tree trunks could have been used as levers, but this seems unlikely as it appears that there were never any forests on the island.

Map of the island showing its chief volcanoes.

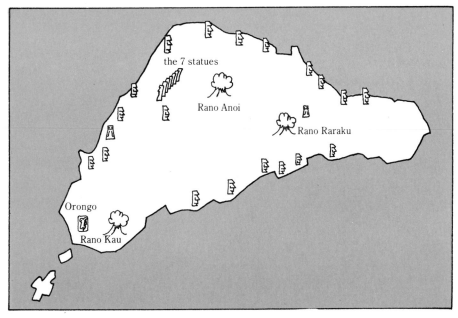

Why did the Romans build an imposing town at Gerasa?

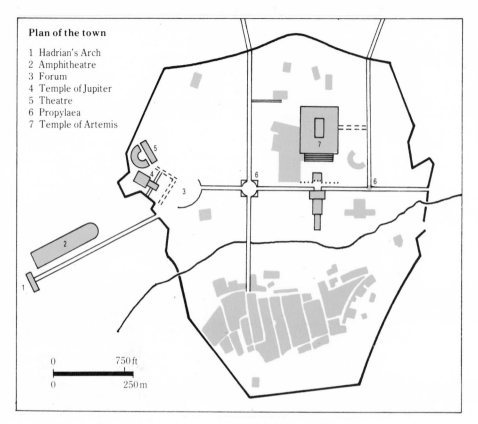

Plan of the town

1 Hadrian's Arch
2 Amphitheatre
3 Forum
4 Temple of Jupiter
5 Theatre
6 Propylaea
7 Temple of Artemis

The Romans, who were brilliant architects and great builders, constructed countless cities throughout the Empire. This reached its peak in the second century BC, when the Roman peace *(Pax Romana)* ruled over the whole Mediterranean basin as far as the north of England, encouraging the development of trade between different provinces.

The Empire became an enormous building site. The Romans, urged on by emperors and local autocrats, created new cities everywhere—in Africa, Syria, the Rhine valley, Gaul and Great Britain. As in Rome, these cities had public baths and gymnasia, sewers and aqueducts, temples, theatres and amphitheatres, triumphal arches, forums and porticos. In other cities, monuments were built as symbols of the grandeur and power of Rome. One of these monumental cities is Jarash (old name Gerasa), the city of a hundred columns!

Gerasa was on the caravan route from Petra. It was so rich that after being destroyed by an earthquake it was rebuilt in a grand manner, in the middle of the first century.

A north-south route *(Cardo Maximus)* and two roads running at right angles to it *(Decumani)* formed the framework. All around it, a network of smaller roads divided the city into a series of zones, blocks and houses, in uniform rectangles. The *Cardo*, which was paved and bordered by an imposing colonnade, turned sharp left on the south side of the town. It eventually met a triumphal arch outside the town. By building an oval forum enclosed by columns, the architects were easily able to disguise this bend in the road. Such a building, the only one of its kind in the Roman world, was intended originally to impress the visitor, and was proof of the city's wealth.

Left: thousands of columns, like those in the forum, used to flank the main roads of Gerasa.

Opposite: the theatre.

Who used to live in the mysterious city of Petra?

In 1812, a Swiss man who had been converted to the Islamic faith decided to make the traditional pilgrimage to Mecca. On the way to the Holy City, his guides told him of the strange ruins which were not far from an Arab village called El Dij, which is in present-day Jordan. He was intrigued by their story and wanted to check what the guides had said. They accompanied him and, at the end of a narrow gorge, he discovered the remains of a strange, lost city, surrounded by barren and jagged mountains.

This is how the ancient city of Petra was rediscovered. Petra is situated half-way between the Dead Sea and the Red Sea and is approached by a series of ravines, in places only 4 m (12 ft) wide between red sandstone cliffs. It was occupied by the Edomites as early as the tenth or ninth century BC, and became the stronghold and treasure city of the Nabataeans in the fourth century BC. The Nabataeans had successfully resisted Antigonus, a successor of Alexander the Great, in 312 BC, and had succeeded in setting up a small independent kingdom which soon controlled the main route taken by caravans crossing the desert.

As a trading centre, Petra was well protected from invasion by the surrounding mountains, and it became the hub of the spice trade from the Far East as early as the Hellenistic period (the period after the death of Alexander the Great).

As a result of its wealth, the city succeeded in avoiding Roman domination until AD 106. It was then united, by the Roman Emperor Trajan, with the province of Arabia.

Among the many remains left by the people of Nabataea are tombs hewn out of the red sandstone cliffs at the entrance to the city. The most beautiful is the Khazne Faroum, the Pharaoh's Treasury, which exhibits a strong Graeco-Roman influence. A Bedouin legend says that when Moses fled from Egypt, the angry Pharaoh dashed off in pursuit. On the way, he stopped and had the Treasury built by magic, to store his gold.

The Roman conquest provided Petra with a forum, paved roads, public baths and a theatre which could seat 3,000 people. In AD 129, Petra received a visit from the emperor Hadrian. But the city's importance was overshadowed by the rise of Palmyra. Shortly after the Arabian conquest in the eighth century, Petra disappeared from human memory.

Plan of the town

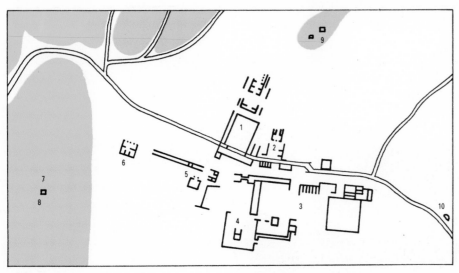

1 Gymnasium
2 Palace
3 Market
4 Great Temple
5 Hot baths, terraces and gardens
6 Khazne Faroum (The Pharaoh's Treasury)
7 Citadel
8 Place of sacrifice
9 Byzantine ruins
10 Theatre

Left: Nabataean tombs at Petra.

Opposite: the Khazne Faroum or 'Pharaoh's Treasury'.

Why are the cities of Cappodocia hidden?

There is a city built mainly underground, hollowed out from tufa (a soft volcanic rock). This city has eight levels, the top one being 75 m (246 ft) from the surface. It has cellars, store-houses, churches, graveyards, mines and ventilation shafts; and it communicates with a neighbouring city by an underground passage, 5 miles (8 km) long!

The city is called Kaymakli, in the heart of Cappodocia in Central Turkey. This is a region of plateaux, which have become so furrowed by erosion that they now consist of a forest of strange-shaped rocks, criss-crossed by many deep valleys and canyons. It is almost a lunar landscape.

But people settled in these remote areas because the valleys were fertile. They hollowed out cave-dwellings in the soft rock and under the ground.

The rise of Christianity during the third century encouraged the settlement here of many Christian families fleeing from persecution by the Romans. Soon hermits, then monks, came to join them. They too were escaping from the evils of the great Byzantine cities, where they were forbidden to worship idols.

These victims of religious persecution also had to protect themselves from increasing attacks by Arabs in this border area between the Byzantine world and

Above: a chapel entrance.

Left: the 'dark church', just one of the thousands of rock churches decorated with cave paintings.

the Islamic world. Everyone, therefore, helped to dig out the soft rock, to form chapels, dining halls and chambers where they could live and worship safe from their attackers.

If you were to climb into a black hole in the side of a rock and switch on your torch, you would be amazed at what you'd see. Everywhere—on the walls, pillars, and ceilings—pictures of Christ and saints with golden haloes look down at you. These are the beautiful frescoes which decorate the underground churches. Several thousand churches have been counted, and nearly two hundred of these still retain their cave-paintings.

Alas, this extraordinary artistic treasure is threatened. Every year erosion and excavation of the rock causes cave-ins. If no rescue measures are undertaken, soon all that we shall have left will be photographs.

Tikal: temple or tomb?

No region in Central America is as inhospitable as the tropical forest of Guatemala where humid heat alternates with frequent torrential rain. But it was in these unlikely surroundings that the Maya civilization was born, at the beginning of the Christian era.

This civilization covered an area which corresponds to present-day Guatemala, British Honduras and Mexican Yucatan. The Maya have left impressive remains throughout this region, which is sometimes called the 'Egypt of the New World'. Built between 300 and 900, the most remarkable of these remains are the temple-pyramids.

These people were only as advanced, technically-speaking, as the Stone Age. They knew nothing about metal, the use of the wheel or animal transport. They used stone tools! But they were advanced in other ways. They used the number zero well before the Indians in India, and they invented the most accurate calendar the human race has ever known. This mysterious people also developed hieroglyphic writing, which has still not been fully deciphered.

The Maya were untiring builders who built very many cities. These cities were not residential, but holy places. A large peasant population lived on the outskirts of the cities, in houses made of perishable materials, which have now disappeared. More than a hundred cities have been counted by archaeologists. Today they are buried under tropical vegetation.

Tikal is one of the oldest cities. The exact date it was established has been found engraved on a stele: 8.12.14.8.5. On our calender that would be 6 July, AD 292. It is also the largest city, with more than 3,000 remains and foundations extending over 6 sq miles (16 sq km). Among these there are many temples and palaces, built on three acropolises. The discovery of engraved steles and altars, instruments, burial chambers, objects of worship, offerings and ornaments have enabled archaeologists to trace the history of this holy place from the sixth century BC to the tenth century AD.

The most remarkable buildings of Tikal are the small temples decorated with engraved bas reliefs, which are perched on top of tall pyramids. The pyramid is made of platforms built in steps one on top of the other. A stone ridge, the width of the temple, tops the whole structure, and emphasizes the carefully thought-out construction of the pyramid. This method of construction made it possible to erect a building which was taller than the biggest trees in the forest. The tallest pyramid is 70 m (230 ft) high. The temple was reached by an extremely steep staircase, with no hand-rail.

For many years it was thought that the Maya pyramid was simply the foundations for the temple. But this was thrown into question by the discovery inside a pyramid of a richly decorated tomb, first at Palenque then at Tikal. In some cases, therefore, the Maya pyramids were tombs, like the Egyptian pyramids. Was there a link between the two civilizations? Here too, many questions remain unanswered.

A temple-pyramid at Tikal. The temple at the top was reached by an extremely steep staircase.

Years of work are still necessary to fully clear the site at Tikal of its tropical foliage.

Why were the two giant Buddhas of Bamian defaced?

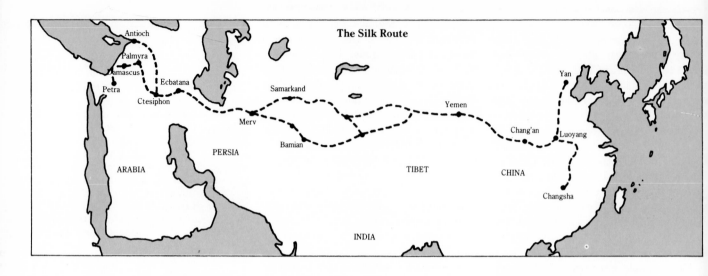

The Silk Route

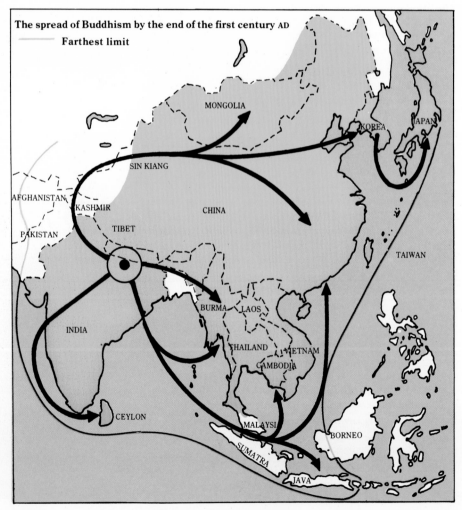

The spread of Buddhism by the end of the first century AD
Farthest limit

Today Afghanistan is Moslem, but between the second and the eighth centuries it was one of the great centres of Buddhism.

This new religion appeared in India, with Buddha as the driving force, in the fifth century BC. Around the beginning of the Christian era it spread rapidly throughout Central Asia, by way of the caravan routes which linked the Mediterranean to the Far East.

The valley of Bamian, a resting place on the Indian section of the Silk Route, thus became one of the great centres of the new faith. The existence of natural grottoes in the soft rock of the cliffs encouraged the setting up of Buddhist monasteries from the third century onwards. Thousands of monks hollowed out cells and shrines connected by galleries, which they decorated with paintings. But the most extraordinary of their artistic works were the giant Buddhas, which they carved in enormous niches, 400 m (1,313 ft) apart.

The smallest Buddha is 35 m (115 ft) tall! Poorly sculpted in the fourth or fifth century, it was probably a 'trial run' for the second, much larger and much later (seventh century) carving.

This second huge statue, standing in a niche decorated with paintings, measures 53 m (174 ft) tall. It is clothed in a monk's habit, with folds which drape gracefully. For a long time, people asked how this effect could be achieved without the use

Above: the cliffs of Bamian. The various rooms hollowed out of the soft rock are connected by galleries.

Right: the great Buddha (53 m; 174 ft high).

Who was Buddha?

Buddha was the son of a king of the Sakya tribe. He was born in India, not far from Benares, in the sixth century BC. According to legend, at the age of twenty-nine he renounced luxuries, left his family and started to live the life of a wandering hermit.

He possessed nothing more than his tunic. After several years' travel and meditation in search of the true way of life, he discovered the mystery of suffering. He learned that the world was full of evil, but that people could triumph over it by understanding and practising goodness.

Now completely 'enlightened', he became a 'buddha' or teacher. He started to preach his beliefs. His fame grew quickly over the whole plain of the Ganges, and he gained very many disciples. His name spread throughout India, to the eastern borders of the Greek world, to China, and over the whole of south-east Asia.

Together with Confucius, who lived at the same time, Buddha remains the greatest of Asia's philosophers.

of scaffolding. How did the sculptors do it? Well, using wooden pegs, they fixed ropes to the walls and coated them with lime mortar overlaid with red paint to form the folds in the cloth. Staircases and galleries were dug out on the inside and the outside to assist them in reaching the top of the statue.

Like so many works of art, the two Buddhas suffered as a result of human rage. In 1221, the town which spread to foot of the cliff was completely flattened on the orders of Genghis Khan. And in the seventeenth century, the canons of the army of the Grand Mogul, Aurengzeb, used the large Buddha as a target!

Why is the basilica of Saint Sophia so famous?

The rulers of olden times all endeavoured to be great builders. This became a devouring passion for Justinian, Emperor of the East (482–565).

He was the great conqueror and the able law-giver concerned with completely recreating the Roman Empire. He built new towns, roads and bridges. The most beautiful monument of his reign was the basilica of Saint Sophia. This was dedicated not to the martyr of that name, but to Divine Wisdom (*sophia* in Greek), that is, to Christ.

The basilica of Saint Sophia was erected in Constantinople on the site of a church of the same name, which had been burned down in 532 during a people's riot. The Emperor ordered it to be rebuilt immediately. He wanted the new shrine to surpass 'anything which had been built since Adam,' to use his own words. One story says that he received the building plans and the necessary money from an angel from heaven.

He called for the most precious materials and the most famous artists in the whole Orient. Ten thousand workmen, divided into a hundred gangs supervised by foremen, undertook its construction; and Justinian personally came to the site daily to advise the architects.

The church, which was completed in 537, is the most impressive monument of Byzantine art. With its vast dome, 33 m (108 ft) wide and 55 m (181 ft) high, it far exceeds other Christian shrines.

It has been shaken several times by earthquakes, and over the centuries the main part has been shored up by strong buttresses which reinforce the building.

Inside the building the mosaics are of a dazzling richness, and the porphyry and marble pillars change from midnight blue to dark green and deep red. How does this happen? By an astonishing play of light. The sun's slanting rays shine on the nave through a circle of windows set in the base of the great dome.

Before it was pillaged in 1204 by the Crusaders when they captured Constantinople, an abundance of precious objects, engraved in gold and silver, added to the dazzling wealth of the church.

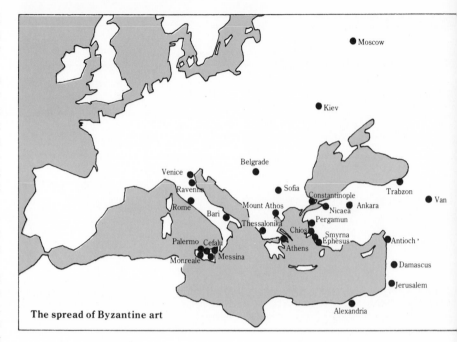

The spread of Byzantine art

Its splendour was so great, that many stories were later told about its construction. It was said that the dome had been built with such light bricks, that twelve of them weighed no more than an ordinary brick! And that the altar had been cast by melting together gold, silver, pearls, precious stones, glass, copper, lead, iron and tin.

Saint Sophia was the centre of the Byzantine world for more than a thousand years. It was then transformed into a mosque in 1453 when the Turks captured the city. The architecture, however, remained intact.

The heaviness of the building disappears when you enter the mosque.

Christ Pantocrator (detail from a mosaic).

Above: Saint Sophia was transformed into a mosque in 1453 when the Turks captured Constantinople. The minarets were added at that time.

The secret of Byzantine mosaics

The Byzantines used both shiny and dull materials to make their mosaics. The shiniest materials they used were the gold or silver tesserae (small cubes). These were made by sticking gold and silver leaf on to a glass base. Other materials that they used, in descending order of brilliance, were enamels (blue, red and green), marbles (white, grey or pink), soft stone and pieces of terracotta.

The tesserae were separately placed on to a bed of wet plaster. This gives Byzantine mosaics an uneven surface, which breaks up the light and produces a constantly changing sheen. The Byzantine artists knew that a background of solid gold would be much too garish and would drown the figures. Therefore, they mixed silver tesserae with the gold tesserae, and also reduced their brilliance by tilting them slightly.

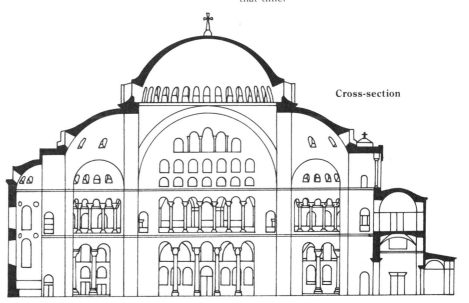

Cross-section

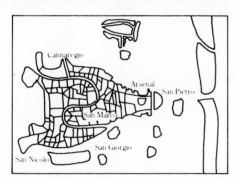

Above: this simplified map shows how the Grand Canal weaves its way across the city.

How was Venice built on water?

The city of Venice was founded in the sixth century AD, and expanded rapidly from the ninth century onwards through sheer human effort. This, one of Christianity's most beautiful and richest cities, was built by crushing hard work, in a desperate struggle against sea and mud.

Originally, Venice was just a number of tiny, sandy islands. These were inhabited by people from the coastal cities, who had found temporary shelter there during the great invasions of the fifth century. It was in 568, with the arrival of the Lombards, that these refugees decided to settle permanently.

The islands stand in the middle of a lagoon, separated from the Adriatic Sea by a narrow, sandy strip. The original Venice was therefore nothing more than a group of straggling villages scattered around a broad channel, which later became the Grand Canal.

The Venetians soon set about increasing the ground area of the most stable islands, by strengthening the banks with intertwined bundles of rushes. These were attached to posts made of larchwood and pine, which would not decay.

Today, Venice is connected to the mainland by a causeway. It rests on millions of pilings driven into the sand. Four hundred humpbacked bridges, which allow boats to pass beneath, span the hundred or so canals dividing the city and linking the various districts. Wells, which have been sunk into reservoirs with watertight walls, supply drinking water. This comes from rain-water which is filtered through sand.

Venice is a city-museum, with hundreds of marble palaces and churches

Left: in Venice, the foundations of buildings consist of very hard wooden piles which will not decay.

Right: laying the foundations;
1 The piles were driven in by 'strikers'.
2 There were two methods of arranging the piles: (a) over the whole ground area for heavy buildings, starting at the outside and working inwards; or (b) in rows if the buildings were less heavy.

1

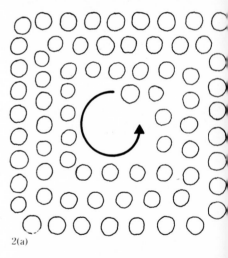

2(a)

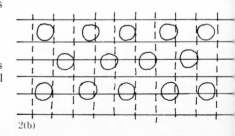

2(b)

Mouth of the Grand Canal, the main waterway
of the city. In the background can be seen the
domes of the church della Salute.

Left: the Bridge of Sighs. More than four hundred bridges connect the various districts of Venice.

Above: a view of the Grand Canal. Many of these palaces belonged to rich merchant families.

reflecting all the styles and periods of European history. But it is balanced very precariously. The Venetians erected a city out of the lagoon by building it on sand and mud, but the problem of keeping it steady has not been completely solved.

Today the city is threatened, simultaneously, by flooding, which occurs with increasing frequency during very high tides and storms; by the ground slowly sinking under the islands; by the micro-organisms which attack the wooden foundations of the buildings; and by air pollution which attacks the marbles and stone facings.

An international rescue is under way in an attempt to cure these problems. May it succeed, and preserve for us this 'Serenissime' Venice, which was once a state in itself.

What causes the Tower of Pisa to lean?

The Tower of Pisa was built, with interruptions, from the eleventh to the fourteenth century. It is a cylindrical, white marble bell-tower, with a beautiful, circular staircase of 292 steps, and it owes its name to its impressive lean to the south. The tower is 55 m (181 ft) high and weighs 14,500 tonne (14,268 ton). It is a monument to the skill of the architects who managed to keep such a large building upright.

Many explanations for this strange tilt have been put forward. One theory is that it is due to an accidental weakening of the ground. Spring water nearby is supposed to have eaten the ground away during construction. Slight alterations were made to the level of the fourth storey to correct the lean, which helped the architects to complete the building.

Another theory is that the tower was built with an intentional tilt, because the architect, Bonnano Pisano, wanted to produce an original piece of work! Although at first this idea seems improbable, it is as well to remember that the work was continued from the third storey, after a hundred-year break because of war. It is obvious that the architects would certainly not have continued to build if they thought that the lean was due to the weak state of the ground. Besides, the building has not been shaken by the many earthquakes which have occurred throughout the centuries, or by the bombing which damaged Pisa during World War II. Does this not prove its stability and its intentional lean?

Whichever explanation you choose to accept, the tower continues to lean, and a strict watch is always kept on it. Although its tilt, which is now 4.31 m (14 ft) from the perpendicular, only increases by 5 mm ($\frac{5}{16}$ in) per year, this would be enough to affect its balance by the end of the century, if no strengthening work were carried out.

Was the lean of the tower of Pisa accidental or intentional? The tilt remains a mystery.

When was the Tower of London built?

Her Majesty's Royal Palace and Fortress of the Tower of London receives about two million visitors each year. They come to marvel at this great castle on the banks of the River Thames, and to explore its turbulent, and at times notorious, history; from the excavations that reveal the development of the fortifications, to the names of the famous, scratched on the walls, who were held prisoner here, and went to their deaths from here. In addition, since the time of Henry III the Tower has been used to store the royal treasure, and people come to see the Crown Jewels, which are housed here.

Although called a tower, the Tower of London is actually a castle consisting of several buildings, towers, and defensive walls. Building began during the reign of William the Conqueror, and reached its peak during the reign of Edward I. Few monarchs used the royal apartments, but the Tower was, and still is, a symbol of the sovereign's power – control of the Tower was considered essential to the control of London – and almost every monarch, from Richard II to James I, spent the night before their Coronation there, and started their Coronation procession from it.

After his victory at the Battle of Hastings in 1066, William the Conqueror proceeded to London for his Coronation. However, London, which at that time was a self-governing city, and which had during the reign of King Stephen claimed the right to elect the king, did not submit quietly to the Conqueror. So he decided that it was necessary to build 'certain strongholds... in the town against the fickleness of the vast and fierce population'.

One of these was constructed on the site of an old Roman fort, close to the Thames beside the old Roman wall, during 1066–67. It consisted of an enclosure surrounded by a ditch and ramparts on the landward side, and it made use of the river and Roman wall as additional defences, and was the beginning of the Tower of London.

However, William needed an imposing fortress, which would symbolize his authority, and which he could also use as a refuge from the population if need be. Work soon began on a great stone keep within the enclosure, which would serve as the military strongpoint and also contain the king's apartments. At the same time, work started on a curtain wall that would surround the tower on the landward sides.

This keep, the Great Tower, started in 1078, was the first stone keep to be built by the Normans in England. Before that time, wood had always been used. It is a square tower with a turret in each corner. It measures 34 m (110 ft) east to west and 37 m (120 ft) north to south. It is about 27 m (90 ft) high. The walls are 5 m (15 ft) thick at the base and 3.5 m (11 ft) thick at the top. The bottom floor contained store-rooms for wood and weapons. The first floor, which was also the floor of entry, housed the Tower guard. The chapel crypt was also on this floor. The second floor contained the rooms used by the Constable of the Tower, by important guests, and on occasions by the king.

William died before the Great Tower was completed, but his son William Rufus finished the building of the Tower and the curtain wall. After this, the Tower remained more or less unchanged for about 100 years, apart from a new wall and outer ditch built by Richard I.

Henry III was the next king to make major additions and alterations to the Tower: to both the defences and the royal apartments. Henry was an unpopular king, and there were many uprisings against him. He needed a power base and refuge in London from which he could defy this opposition. Preferring the Tower to the palace at Westminster, because it was more secure, he greatly strengthened and improved its defences, and made frequent use of it, elevating the Tower to the role of a major royal palace.

The area of the Tower was extended in all three directions on the landward side and a new outer, towered wall and moat were constructed. A guard-wall with a

The Tower of London seen from the banks of the River Thames.

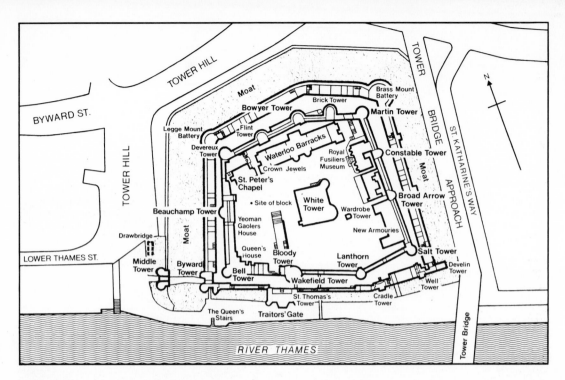

Ground plan of the Tower of London as it is today. Many additions have been made since the first defensive building was erected on this site in 1078, by William the Conqueror.

water-gate set into it was built along the river. At the same time, the inner buildings were greatly strengthened. These extensions to the Tower were very unpopular, and when, during work on the outer wall, part of it collapsed, in 1240 and again in 1241, the citizens of London were delighted.

The royal apartments in the Great Tower had hardly ever been used, and Henry built a new palace within the inner area of the Tower. He loved beauty and elegance, and the new apartments were sumptuously decorated. The Queen's rooms were wainscoted and white-washed, and painted with flowers. The King's Chamber was whitewashed, and new window-shutters, decorated with the royal coat-of-arms, were fitted. The walls of the King's Privy Chamber were decorated with frescoes depicting the story of Antiochus the Great. In addition, new kitchens were built and the Chapel was refurbished.

The most striking change made during Henry's reign, however, was the whitewashing of the Great Tower, and following this it was renamed the White Tower.

In 1272 Edward I succeeded his father, Henry III, and he continued to develop and improve the Tower's defences, so that by the time of his death in 1285, the Tower

had reached the fullest extent of its development as a medieval castle.

The ditch that had been dug during Henry's reign was filled in, another encircling wall was built outside Henry's, and a new moat was dug beyond that. Land was reclaimed along the river frontage and a new towered wall was constructed along the river's edge, with a new water-gate, called Traitor's Gate as it was the entrance by which prisoners were brought into the Tower. The water-gate in the inner wall was converted to a land-gate, and a tower was built over it that later came to be known as the Bloody Tower. All the entrances to the Tower were fortified.

Why were so many encircling walls built around the Tower? They were added in response to changes in methods of warfare and theories of defence. When the early parts of the Tower were built, castle defence depended on a strong central keep. By the time Edward I came to the throne, castle defences had become far more elaborate and depended on a series of encircling walls, around an inner group of buildings none of which could be attacked directly. This arrangement provided for more effective protection to the central stronghold from mining and other seige techniques.

With the additions that Edward I made,

the White Tower became the central feature in a complicated arrangement of inner and outer defensive walls, and despite later additions and modifications and the restoration work of the nineteenth century, the Tower remains the most complete example of medieval castle architecture in Britain.

Prisoners in the Tower

It was during Tudor times that the Tower acquired its reputation as an infamous prison and the scene of murder and torture. However, it had been used as a prison in medieval times also, as were all castles. Prisoners were kept in several different buildings within the Tower, and many famous names are scratched into the walls.

The Bloody Tower is associated with the 'Princes in the Tower', Edward V and Richard, Duke of York; Thomas Cranmer, Archbishop of Canterbury; Sir Walter Raleigh; Robert Carr, Earl of Somerset; William Laud, Archbishop of Canterbury. The Bell Tower was associated with Sir Thomas More, and Princess Elizabeth (later Elizabeth I); the Wakefield Tower with Henry VI; the Lieutenant's Lodgings (now the Queen's House) with Anne Boleyn; the Gentlemen Gaoler's House with Lady Jane Grey; and the Bowyer Tower with George, Duke of Clarence.

Machu-Picchu—an Inca fortress or refuge?

Not far from Cuzco, in Peru, the ruins of Machu-Picchu, the lost city of the Incas, rise 2,000 m (6,564 ft) above sea-level. They sit on a rocky spur which overlooks the river Urubamba. It is a setting of awe-inspiring beauty.

This well-preserved, fortified city is difficult to reach and was completely unknown to the Spanish conquistadors, who captured the Inca Empire in 1537. It was rediscovered in 1911 by Hiram Birgham, an American professor at Yale University. Whilst looking for the tomb of the last emperor, he came by chance upon this eagle's eyrie—one of the most mysterious wonders of the world.

Machu-Picchu was constructed of granite blocks, which were smoothed and shaped using wet sand. They were joined together perfectly, without the use of mortar. The city was built on steeply-sloping ground and is 400 m (1,313 ft) long by 200 m (656 ft) wide. It follows the contours of the land and forms an integral part of the mountain. However, it retains the typical lay-out of an Inca city, with an upper town reserved for important townspeople, and a lower town occupied by the rest of the population. The city was built around a central square and many

small, stepped streets connected the different districts: farming, military, public, political, religious and residential.

The residential district was composed of about 150 rectangular stone houses. They had thick walls, narrow windows

The temple of the 'Three Windows' is one of the most remarkable examples of Inca architecture. Notice how big the blocks of stone are, and how perfect the joints. Many Inca building techniques have still not been explained.

Plan of the town

0   50   100 m

1 Residential district
2 Terraces under cultivation
3 Ceremonial square
4 Intihuatana (sun calendar)
5 Temple district
6 Royal palace
7 Tower

and doors, and steeply-sloping thatched roofs, to shed the rain easily—rain is plentiful in this very humid region. Some houses had two stories, and have retained their gable ends. On the west side of the main square, there is a series of buildings which are thought to have been temples.

Hundreds of terraces were built to the north and south, on the steeply-sloping mountainside. These terraces were supported by strong walls and were intended for the growth of crops. They were connected by steps, and were watered from a network of stone-filled channels.

It must have required super-human effort to build Machu-Picchu. Yet the city did not play a large part in the political and economic life of the Inca Empire, and its population could never have been more than one thousand.

Why, then, was it built? One theory is that it was built as a refuge for the Inca emperor. Another theory is that Machu-Picchu was merely a look-out post for keeping an eye on the tribes of the Amazonian forest, whose raids into the heart of the Empire were always dangerous.

The site was certainly important from a military point of view. Surrounded by deep chasms and strengthened at weak points by stone walls 6 m (20 ft) high, the city was an impenetrable fortress which, thanks to its crops, was able to feed its inhabitants. Its strategic position meant that it could control a large part of the Urubamba valley.

Today, this archaeological site still guards the secrets of its beginnings, purpose and its final neglect. We shall never know why this extraordinary city existed.

General view of the city, showing its imposing position.

How were the faience tiles of the Royal Mosque at Isfahan produced?

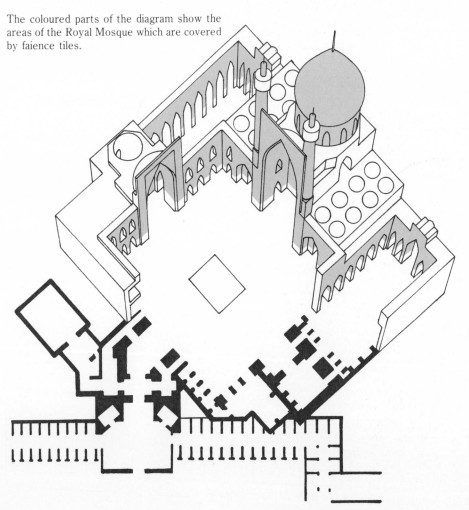

The North door (detail).

The coloured parts of the diagram show the areas of the Royal Mosque which are covered by faience tiles.

The city of Isfahan, with its countless minarets and domes covered in glowing coloured tiles, is a green oasis set in the heart of a barren desert plateau.

This city was the capital of the Persian Empire under the Safavid dynasty in the seventeenth century. It rapidly became famous in Europe from the stories told by travellers and merchants, who had been received at the Royal Court there. They described the wonderful new city, which had been built to the south-west of the old town.

Isfahan was the work of Shah Abbas I (1587–1626), and was constructed to a simple but imposing town plan.

A vast royal square, 512 m (1,680 ft) by 159 m (522 ft), planned by the sovereign as a polo ground, and surrounded by arcaded buildings, formed the heart of the town.

On the east side of the square, facing the Royal Palace with its covered terrace, Shah Abbas built a mosque decorated with ceramics, both on the inside and outside, and with magnificent decorative carpets with geometric designs in gold on a turquoise-blue background. Shah Abbas soon decided that this building was too small for Court pageantry, and had another more spacious mosque built in haste on the south side of the square. This mosque has become a wonder of the world, because of the faience tiles which cover its walls, minarets, cupolas and internal courtyards.

The King was afraid that he would never see the finished building. He therefore forced the architects to use painted and glazed tiles, which could be produced more quickly and more easily, in place of the delicate ceramic mosaics.

The decorative panels were produced on a white background made from several tiles 23 sq cm (60 sq in) and 2 cm (1 in) thick. A draughtsman used a black brush to draw the outline of various arabesque designs, which were then painted in. The tiles were then fired. This process, using techniques perfected in the twelfth century, involved at least two firings; the first for the white surfaces, and the second for the coloured surfaces.

The King's Mosque was finished in 1629 after eighteen years' work. Twenty million bricks and a million faience tiles were used. It is one of the wonders of Safavid art. Its ornamentation, with Beauty as the ideal, symbolizes a paradise already present here on Earth.

Opposite: the bulb-shaped dome.

Is the Taj-Mahal a mosque?

When his father, Jehangir, died in 1627, Shah Jehan, the fifth Emperor of the Mogul dynasty, inherited a vast empire which covered the major part of the Indian peninsula. His wife, Mumtazi Mahal, the 'Pearl of the Palace', whom he loved passionately, gave him strong support in his duty.

Shah Jehan, in the tradition of his predecessors, was a great builder. Under his reign (1627–1658), Mogul architecture reached a peak of elegance and magnificence, and its most famous monument, the Taj-Mahal, was built. But this was in fact a monument of sorrow.

Shah Jehan was heart-broken when his beloved wife died when their fourteenth child was born. He vowed to erect a tomb to her, which would be more beautiful than anything the world had known. To do this, he brought artists from Persia, Arabia, Turkey, and even from France and Italy. He chose a site in the capital, Agra, beside the river Yamura. Twenty thousand masons worked unceasingly for twenty-two years, to build a mausoleum of white marble encrusted with semi-precious stones.

The mausoleum was erected on a marble terrace, which itself stood on an enormous platform of red sandstone, decked with gardens.

Who were the Grand Moguls?

This was the name given to Indian rulers, who were not Moguls, but Turks descended from Tamerlane. The Mogul Empire was founded by Baber, who destroyed the sultanate of Delhi in 1526. His dynasty ruled India for three centuries, and reached the peak of its glory under the great reigns of Akbar (1556–1605), Jehangir (1605–1627), Shah Jehan (1627–1658) and Aurengzeb (1658–1707). It then declined rapidly as the result of dynastic quarrels. The Moguls were great conquerors and skilled administrators. They heped to bring Moslem art to India, among which there are many masterpieces.

This 'dreamy marvel', as Francis de Croiset described it (see box opposite), is crowned by a majestic dome, surrounded by four small cupolas. Four minarets, each 42 m (138 ft) high, border the terrace. The entire building is inlaid in complicated patterns, with lapis lazuli, jasper, agate, turquoise and rubies. A golden barrier encrusted with precious stones (which today has been replaced by delicately chiselled marble) surrounded the tomb, while fine golden curtains hung from the vaults of the building.

Shah Jehan wanted to be buried on the other bank of the river in an identical tomb, which would be connected to his wife's tomb by a bridge spanning the river. But he was deposed and imprisoned in 1658 by his son, Aurengzeb, who was known for his harsh character. Shah Jehan was finally buried in 1666 beside Mumtazi, in the Taj Mahal.

It is said this mausoleum of love is even more beautiful by moonlight.

A travelling writer's impression of the Taj-Mahal:

'...The light plays with the smooth planes and recesses of its vast, polished surfaces. It moves, it really appears to move. It turns on its pedestal. There is nothing behind it, apart from the sky: it seems ready to take off.'

Francis de Croisset,
Nous avons fait un beau voyage
(Grasset, 1930).

What are the important symbols of the Palace of Versailles?

'Versailles! Palace of the Sun! A poem of ornament, greenery and water!' This is how a writer of the time described the palace which Louis XIV was prompted to build on the model of the castle of Vaux-le-Vicomte, after he had attended a feast there, given in his honour by his financial secretary, Nicolas Fouquet.

Versailles, 16 miles (25 km) south-west of Paris, is a regal creation. It is built on a small hillock, overlooking the town of Versailles on one side and the gardens on the other. In the reign of his father, Louis XIII, it was only a simple hunting lodge, but during Louis XIV's reign it became a showy palace, 400 m (1,313 ft) long, the largest ever built in Europe.

The transformation of the small brick and stone lodge into a vast stone and marble palace was carried out in several stages, under the King's personal supervision.

The architect Le Vau, the painter Le Brun and the gardener Le Nôtre, who had created the castle at Vaux-le-Vicomte, were chosen by Louis XIV to carry out the work at Versailles. They started in 1661 under the direction of Le Vau, who drew up the general plan incorporating the hunting lodge, which was to form the main part of the palace. As the buildings appeared too symmetrical, statues, busts, columns and balustrades were placed on the wings to soften the appearance. In 1678, the King appointed the architect Mansart to add two enormous wings to the north and south of the palace.

Despite being urged by his chief advisor, Colbert, to stay at the Louvre, the King decided to make Versailles the background setting for his reign, and he moved his court there in 1682.

Versailles was not only the official residence of the King; it also became a symbol of the glory and importance of his sovereignity.

The characteristics of the design and decoration of the palace were dignity, symmetry and restraint. Large windows let sunlight into the palace to show off to advantage the gold decorations of the apartment. This shimmering and brilliant effect was further accentuated by the use of countless mirrors. Indeed, everything combined to create a fairy-tale beauty. The lightness of the internal decoration was emphasized by the contrast with the dark, distant foliage of the park.

The King's Bedchamber, at the very centre of the palace, represents the sun in the universe. Everything revolves around it, and everything starts at this important point.

This worship of light is not only intended as a decorative theme. It is important to realize that by building Versailles, the King wanted to remind the world that he received his power from God. This power is also identified with the sun. If there were no sun, there would be no life. For this reason, one single idea dominates the furnishings of the palace: the glorification of the Sun-King in all forms of art. This is why the sun is a theme running through the decoration of the palace. Apollo, who drives the chariot of the sun in Greek mythology, is a favourite subject for the paintings and sculptures.

Nothing escaped the King's attention. The ponds of water-lilies are decorated at the four corners with statues which represent the four largest rivers in France. Statues of nymphs and small river-gods stand between them. Three roads meet at the royal stables in front of the palace—the middle one leads to Paris and

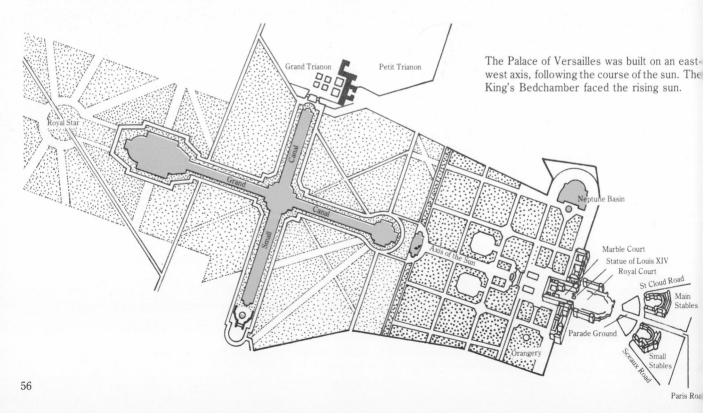

The Palace of Versailles was built on an east-west axis, following the course of the sun. The King's Bedchamber faced the rising sun.

the other two to Saint Cloud and Sceaux. The palace, therefore, stands symbolically between the river- and land-routes of the kingdom.

This theme of centralization in the design of the palace was taken up by many foreign monarchs, such as Ludwig II of Bavaria. Throughout the nineteenth century they constructed residences, taking Versailles as their model.

The arms of France decorate the front of the Gate of Honour.

The gardens were designed by Le Nôtre.

Shrove-tide festivities of 1683

'I had not been to Versailles for two or three years. So I went to see the King's grand apartment, which had been recently built, the large gathering of people, and the illuminations which take place three times a week, and which I had heard much about. Nothing in the world can be so beautiful, so magnificent, or so astonishing. The entrance hall, the drawing room, the bedchambers, the gallery and the study at the far end are of enormous length. Imagine the effect of a thousand candles in this grand suite of apartments. I thought that everything was ablaze. Even the full sun in the month of July does not shine so brilliantly. The gold and silver furnishings still had their special brilliance, as did the gilding and the marbles. All the decorations were rich and sumptuous. There were tapestries, statues, pictures, silverware, vases, flowers, braziers, chandeliers, candlesticks, door curtains, carpets, all different and all exceptional.'

Anonymous

The Marble Court and the royal apartments. The three central windows are those of the King's Bedchamber.

Overleaf: the main façade overlooking the gardens, the symbolic statue of the river Seine in the foreground.

What was the Eiffel Tower built to celebrate?

upper balcony
beacon balcony
third stage
350m² (1,256ft²)

intermediate stage

312.27m (1,025ft)

second stage
1,570m² (5,633ft²)

first stage
4,200m²
(15,070ft²)

—124.90m (410ft)—

Plan of the elevation of the Eiffel Tower
(after Gustave Eiffel)

In France in 1885, the government of the Third Republic decided to celebrate the first centenary of the French Revolution, by organizing an International Exhibition in Paris for 1889. The main attraction would be a 300m (985ft) high tower. Among the designs considered was one from an engineer who would become world-famous for his metal structures: Gustave Eiffel.

Eiffel suggested building a four-sided pyramid-shaped tower with three stories. It would weigh a total of 7,000 tonne (6,888ton). The construction would be light and open, in order to withstand the force of the wind.

The design was accepted and work began in 1887 on the Champ-de-Mars, not far from the Seine.

First of all, sixteen supports were erected to form the feet of the tower (four per foot), which face north, south, east and west. These supports rested on steel bases, which had been fixed into a bed of concrete by two bolts, 8m (26ft) long and 10cm (4in) in diameter. Each support was fitted with an hydraulic jack for adjusting the level of the first stage, which would connect the four legs. (The jacks

were removed when the construction work was finished, and have since been replaced by chocks). The hundred connection holes fitted together without a single touch of the file or the slightest alteration.

The tower was built in two years, two months and two days, by only sixty workmen. It is made up of 15,000 pieces fixed together with 2½ million rivets. Each piece was individually designed down to the smallest detail, and was manufactured and pre-assembled in Eiffel's workshop at Levallois-Perret. They were then transported to the Champ-de-Mars and put straight into place. The framework was constructed with mathematical precision. Logarithmic calculations were used which was revolutionary at that time. The pieces were drilled with such precision that all the workmen had to do was bolt them into place.

Eiffel was particularly concerned about his workmen's safety. So he installed a system of temporary floors, guard-rails and fencing, which allowed his 'builders in the sky' to work in complete safety. Indeed, no accidents occurred during the construction work.

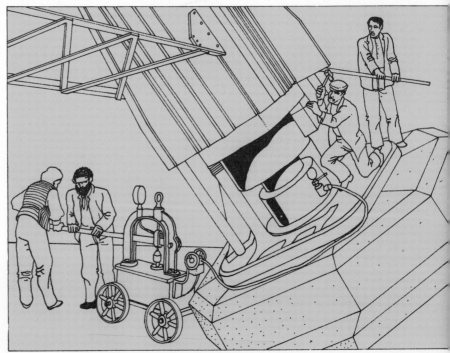

The calculations for the Eiffel Tower were so precise that the hydraulic jacks, incorporated into the base of each column to adjust the level of the first platform, were never used.

There were many critics of the tower during its construction, particularly among artists and writers of the time. But the main objections came from scientists, who tried to show, using skilful calculations, that the tower could get no higher than 221 m (725 ft). Besides, they argued, the structure would sway and collapse in the first strong wind. But the tower still stands today.

In fact Gustave Eiffel's design made allowance for a sway of 30 cm (12 in) without any danger. Generally, the tower sways no more then 12 cm (5 in) in a strong wind. The greatest variation ever observed (18 cm; 7 in) was due to the expansion of the metal parts exposed to the sun!

Eiffel's work is now an essential part of the Parisian landscape. For more than half a century it was the tallest tower in the world, but it has now been overtaken by the CN Tower in Metro Centre, Toronto, Canada, which measures 553 m (1,815 ft).

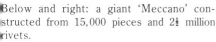

Below and right: a giant 'Meccano' constructed from 15,000 pieces and 2½ million rivets.

Critics of the Eiffel Tower

'We are writers, painters, sculptors, architects and lovers of the beauty of Paris, which until now has remained untouched. We wish to protest with all our might and indignation against the erection of the useless and monstrous Eiffel Tower in the heart of our capital. We do this in the name of French taste, which has gone unappreciated, and in the name of art and French history, which is threatened [...] One only has to imagine a ridiculous tower, which makes you feel giddy, and which dominates Paris like a giant, black factory-chimney. Its bulk dwarfs the Notre Dame, Sainte Chapelle, Saint-Jacques' Tower, the Louvre, the Dome des Invalides and the Arc de Triomphe. All our monuments will be made to feel small, all our architecture will be dwarfed and disappear in this ghastly dream. For twenty years we shall see the abominable shadow of the abominable column of bolted metal spreading like an ink-stain over the whole city—a city which still quivers with the spirit of centuries.'

This surprising pamphlet was signed by Gounod, Garnier, Alexandre Dumas, François Coppée, Leconte de Lisle, Sully-Prudhomme, Maupassant, Meissonier, Huysmans etc.

How did the faces of four American presidents appear on the side of Mount Rushmore?

In the Black Hills of South Dakota, USA, the faces of four of the country's presidents gaze out over the surrounding countryside. They are the faces of George Washington, Thomas Jefferson, Abraham Lincoln, and Theodore Roosevelt: men who turned their dreams for America into reality. They are honoured in this national memorial carved into the south-eastern face of Mount Rushmore; the inspiration and work of sculptor Gutzon Borglum.

Borglum had always believed that America should have a national memorial of heroic proportions, and in 1923 he got his chance to create one. The director of the South Dakota Historical Society suggested that a monumental sculpture should be carved on Mount Rushmore, a 1,745m (5,725ft) mountain whose south-east face consisted of bare granite.

In 1925, the idea was given government approval and the mountain was established as a national memorial.

It had originally been suggested that a group of western heroes be carved there, but Borglum thought that the four presidents would be more appropriate.

Borglum first made plaster models of the faces. Each was to measure 18m (60ft) from forehead to chin; the equivalent of a six-storey building. Then he began to plan out the sculpture on the rock-face by dropping plumb lines from the top of the mountain.

The work of carving out the faces began in August 1927. The mountain was continually shaken by the blasting of dynamite and the roar of jack-hammers. And in 1930 the first face, that of George Washington, was finished, and was dedicated on 4 July of that year.

Borglum trained teams of miners to work with him. They worked from specially-constructed scaffolding, while he darted about overseeing the work and checking the effects of the light at different times of the day on the faces as they emerged.

The work progressed intermittently until Borglum died in March 1941, and the project was finally completed in October of that year by Borglum's son Lincoln. During the fourteen years that the work lasted, 408,000 tonne (450,000 ton) of rock were removed from the mountain face.

This monumental sculpture was carved from the bare granite rock on the south-east face of Mount Rushmore, in the Black Hills of South Dakota.

The Mount Rushmore National Memorial celebrates four American presidents. They are, from left to right, George Washington, Thomas Jefferson, Theodore Roosevelt and Abraham Lincoln.

Many tributes have been paid to the Mount Rushmore National Memorial, but the words of architect Frank Lloyd Wright, describe most accurately this awe-inspiring work: 'The noble countenances emerge as though the spirit of the mountain heard a human plan and itself became a human countenance'.

Why did skyscrapers originate in New York?

On 28 July 1945, a B25 bomber of the US Air Force, lost in the fog over New York, crashed head-on, at more than 249 miles (400 km) per hour, into the Empire State Building. This building, which was the tallest in the world and which had been designed to withstand strong winds, was hardly damaged, despite the tremendous shock.

Construction of the Empire State Building.

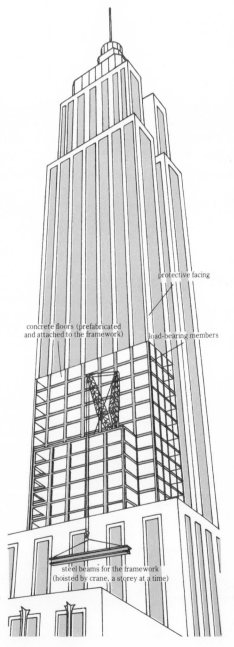

protective facing

concrete floors (prefabricated and attached to the framework)

load-bearing members

steel beams for the framework (hoisted by crane, a storey at a time)

The Empire State Building is a type of building known as a skyscraper. The skyscraper originated in the United States of America at the end of the last century. Its appearance coincided with the invention of the lift by an American, Elisha Graves Otis, and with the increasing use of steel and concrete in architecture.

The skyscraper was chiefly designed as a practical building. It has one great advantage over traditional buildings: it can concentrate a larger number of people into the same ground area. This made it a popular architectural design as there was a shortage of land in large city centres, such as New York. As they could no longer expand sideways on the island of Manhattan, the architects resolved the problem by building upwards. The sub-soil of New York is made up of hard rock, which is suitable for this type of building.

The first skyscraper appeared on the New York skyline in 1902. Banks, insurance companies and large firms chose this new architecture, and soon Manhattan became a forest of skyscrapers.

The structure of these new monsters is quite simple: a steel framework supports concrete floors and glass walls. Brickwork covers the metal skeleton to protect it against corrosion.

The Empire State Building, standing at 381 m (1,250 ft) high, broke all records in 1932. Its 102 stories were built in seventeen months, at a rate of six per month! It required 60,000 tonne (59,040 ton) of steel, 6,500 windows, 3,480 miles (5,600 km) of telephone cable and 597 miles (960 km) of water-pipes. Strict organization of the construction work meant that the concrete, steel and bricks required were all ready and available at the same time to the 3,500 workmen.

In 1950, a TV tower was added to the Empire State Building, bringing its height to 448 m (1,470 ft). Today, seventy-two lifts serve the building, and transport the 25,000 people who work in it!

The largest skyscraper in the world is the Sears Building in Chicago. The building itself is 443 m (1,454 ft) high, and the addition of two TV antennae bring its total height to 475 m (1,559 ft).

At the heart of New York lies the island of
Manhattan. Here, several generations of skyscraper stand side by side.

Why have the Brazilians moved their capital?

Brasilia, the capital of Brazil, lies 1,200 m (3,938 ft) above sea-level, at the heart of the Brazilian plateau, in a region which is almost devoid of people. Its position is no accident for it was built here as the result of a deliberate decision.

Previously Brazil's largest cities, Bahia, Rio de Janeiro (then the capital) and Sao Paulo, were positioned on the Atlantic coast. They were an inheritance from the Portuguese colonial period. After the country's independence in 1822, heads of state saw the need to build a new capital inland, to attract an ever-growing population from the coast, and to encourage the development of the high plateaux. When Kubitschek became President of the Republic in 1956, he decided to put this old dream into effect.

A competition was announced, to find the person who could design the most beautiful plan for the city of the future. It was to be situated in the middle of the desert. Twenty-six designs were submitted in all, and the members of the judging panel chose the plans designed by Lucio Costa.

His design is simple. It follows the outline of a cross, to symbolize the spread of civilization inland. From this basic outline, the town has developed around two large dividing lines or axes.

The Great Axis, 4 miles (6 km) long, ends at a triangular square known as Three Powers' Square. It is bordered by government offices designed by the architect Oscar Niemeyer. The other axis, 6 miles (10 km) long, bends to take in the curve of an artificial lake. It connects with the arterial road, where the residential and business areas are. At the intersection of these two dividing lines, there is an enormous platform with offices, shops, hotels and leisure centres. This is the centre of the city.

At the end of the Great Axis, the vast Three Powers' Square forms the main part of the city and is a symbol of the centralization of power in the new capital. Three buildings, standing at each corner of the Square at equal distances apart, represent the Executive Power (the Senate), the Judicial Power (the Palace of Justice) and the Legislative Power (the Congress). The first two stand at the base of the triangle, the third at the apex. These buildings are overlooked by two twenty-eight storey skyscrapers, which house the administrative departments of the Congress. A little further on, beside the lake, the original style of the President's residence, the Palace of the Dawn, is reflected on the water's surface.

You can see that fantasy rules in Brasilia, both from the overall plan of the city and from the architecture and position of the public buildings.

The architect, Oscar Niemeyer, has freely expressed his genius, particularly in his design of the theatre (a squat pyramid) and of the cathedral. The cathedral's twenty-one concrete pillars, connected by panes of glass, form a circle 70 m (230 ft) in diameter, that suggests an ascent into infinity.

Brasilia was commenced in 1960, and now has a population of 400,000. The people have not been forgotten in this city of the future. Good sense and the spectacular have been combined effectively in the design of the city. For example, cars

Map to show how Brasilia radiates outwards

and pedestrians move around in harmony but on roads at different levels.

As with anything new, Brasilia has its critics, both at home and abroad. It is often criticized for being cold and monotonous. But in the future, when it can be seen in perspective, justice will be done to this wonder of modern town-planning.

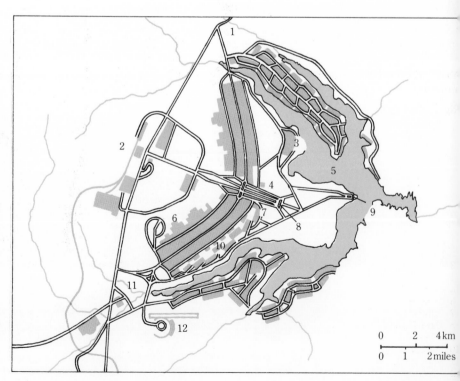

Above: the Palace of Congress with its two inverted domes.

Right: the interior of the cathedral.

Opposite: plan of the city.

 1 Botanical garden
 2 Station
 3 Residential area
 4 University/Ministries
 5 Lake Brasilia
 6 Cemetery
 7 Cathedral
 8 Three Powers' Square
 9 Palace of the Dawn
10 Embassies
11 Zoo
12 Airport

How do you cross the Bosporus today?

From the earliest times, the journey from Europe to Asia was made by boat. Only two people, the Persian, Xerxes, and the Macedonian, Alexander the Great, succeeded in making pontoon bridges across the Bosporus Strait, to enable their armies to cross between the two continents.

Today, in the centre of Istanbul (formerly called Constantinople), a suspension bridge spans the strait, uniting European and Asiatic Turkey. The Europa Bridge is a vital link in the route between Istanbul and Ankara, the present capital in the heart of Asiatic Turkey.

The bridge was planned towards the end of World War II, but was finally opened to traffic in 1973, after three years' construction. It was designed to withstand earthquakes, which often occur in this area, and it is an impressive structure of exceptional elegance.

After the Humber Bridge in Britain, it is the largest suspension bridge in Europe. It is 1,560 m (5,120 ft) long: the central span alone is 1,074 m (3,525 ft). This magnificent piece of work consists of a roadway, 30 m (99 ft) wide, made up of sixty prefabricated sections, each weighing 150 tonne (148 ton). These are suspended by cables supported from 165 m (542 ft) high steel pylons. The two stout suspension cables are anchored on both sides of the bridge in particularly large beds of concrete (50 m; 164 ft thick).

Each suspension cable is made up of 10,412 twisted steel ropes. Placed end to end, they would stretch for 24,856 miles (40,000 km), once around the world!

The Europa Bridge is the only bridge in the world which joins two continents. Could a bridge, spanning the Straits of Gibraltar, connect Europe to Africa by the year 2000?

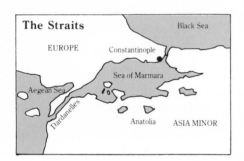

The Straits

Black Sea
EUROPE
Constantinople
Sea of Marmara
Aegean Sea
Dardanelles
Anatolia
ASIA MINOR

The longest suspension bridges in the world

These figures are based on the distance between the piers. The order is as follows:

1) Humber Bridge (Great Britain)
1,380 m (4,529 ft)
2) Verrazano Bridge, New York (USA)
1,298 m (4,260 ft)
3) Golden Gate Bridge, San Francisco (USA)   1,280 m (4,201 ft)
4) Mackirac Bridge, State of Michigan (USA)   1,158 m (3,801 ft)
5) Europa Bridge (Turkey)
1,074 m (3,525 ft)

Cross-section

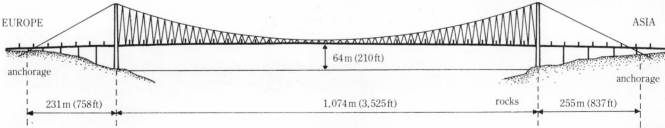

EUROPE   ASIA

64 m (210 ft)

anchorage   anchorage

231 m (758 ft)   1,074 m (3,525 ft)   rocks   255 m (837 ft)

The Europa Bridge joins Europe and Asia. Its
central span is more than 1 km (3,525 ft) long!

Which is the strangest opera house in the world?

The Grand Opera House in Sydney, Australia, was declared open by Queen Elizabeth II in 1973. It is one of the most original architectural works of this century.

The building, which is surrounded on three sides by the sea, stands at the harbour entrance, close to the spot where the first British settlers landed in 1788.

The Opera House was designed in 1957 by the Danish architect, Joern Utzon. Three gigantic structures resembling wind-filled sails, stand on a vast concrete platform, which covers an area of 2 hectares (5 acres), with a massive staircase leading up to them. One of these structures is the concert hall (2,700 seats), the second is the opera house (1,550 seats), and the third, the smallest, is a restaurant.

It took fourteen years to complete this massive cultural complex and, during that time, enormous changes were made to the original design. Architects and engineers had to solve many technical problems, concerning the building of the shells.

After much research, they finally decided to use a framework of sections 5 m (16 ft) long, made of prefabricated concrete. Each section interlocked with the next. These were hoisted into place using giant cranes. A temporary metal frame supported each completed arch, until it was attached to the next.

More than a million white ceramic tiles cover the entire building. These tiles were stuck on to panels of prefabricated concrete riveted to the framework. The largest were 10 m (33 ft) long and 2.5 m (8 ft) wide, and weighed 4 tonne (approximately 4 ton).

This unusual theatre, which cost 102 million Australian dollars to build, was paid for by a lottery organized to raise the money. It is the only one of its kind in the world.

The Sydney Opera House is a wonder of engineering, which heralds the twenty-first century.

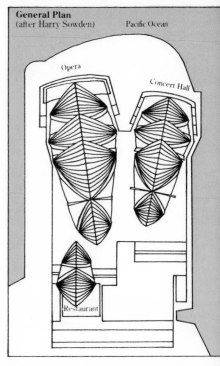

General Plan
(after Harry Sowden)   Pacific Ocean

Opera   Concert Hall

Restaurant

Below and opposite: more than a million white ceramic tiles cover the shells of the Sydney Opera House. The tallest of these shells measures 67 m (220 ft).

Glossary

Acanthus: foliage of a plant used in the decorative design of a **Corinthian capital**.

Altar: table of sacrifice.

Amphitheatre: a building with rows of tiered seats, around an open space.

Apadana: audience hall.

Arabesque: Arabian decorative design of intertwined lines.

Basilica: in antiquity, a public hall or courtroom with aisles. From the fourth century, Christian churches built on a similar ground plan were also called basilicas.

Buttress: a block of stonework to reinforce or **buttress** a wall.

To buttress: to support a wall with buttresses to counteract outward pressure.

Capital: a stone crowning the shaft of a column, pillar or **pilaster**.

Cella: in antiquity, a place in the temple where the statue of the god was placed.

Citadel: a fortress in or near a city.

Classicism: a style characteristic of ancient Greece and Rome.

Colonnade: a series of columns with **entablature**.

Corinthian: see **order**.

Cupola: small, rounded dome.

Doric: see **order**.

Entablature: part of an **order**, above the column.

Façade: in architecture, any exterior face of a building.

Faience: glazed pottery of eastern origin.

Forum: in Roman times, a square where public business was transacted.

Fresco: a wall painting using water colours on wet plaster.

Frieze: part of the **entablature**, often decorated with sculpted figures.

Ionic: see **order**.

Lintel: horizontal timber or stone over door or opening.

Minaret: a slender tower connected to a mosque, from which the call to prayer is given.

Opisthodomos: enclosed space at the rear of the **cella** in a Greek temple.

Order: in architecture, one of the different ways in which the column and its **entablature**, with their various parts, are moulded and related to each other.

Greek architecture has three orders: Doric (the oldest, sturdiest and simplest);

Ionic (characterized by the ornamental scrolls on its **capitals**);

Corinthian (the most ornate of the three orders with **acanthus** leaf decoration on its capitals).

The Romans added the Tuscan order (debased Doric) and the Composite order (a mixture of Ionic and Corinthian).

Pilaster: a rectangular column slightly projecting from the wall where it stands.

Portico: roofed open space, with columns, arches or pillars, used for shelter or as a covered walk.

Pronaos: rear part of a temple.

Propylaeum: a large porch.

Relief: moulded or carved figures or decorative designs projecting from the background. Low or bas relief projects a little way; middle- or half-relief projects halfway; high relief projects almost entirely.

Sarcophagus: stone or marble tomb.

Stele: upright slab or pillar with carved inscription.

Stereobate: lower part of a building without ornamental mouldings.

Stucco: plaster which imitates marble.

Stylobate: base supporting a row of columns.

Volute: spiral scroll used as decorative design on an **Ionic** column.

Acknowledgements

All photographs by Jean-Marc Durou and Joël Jaffre, with the exception of: British Tourist Authority pp 17 (below) and 47; Diafrance pp 27 and 28; Jeanmet pp 44 (above and left) and 45; Susan Lund p 60; Ministère de Tourisme et d'Information de Turquie pp 41 (right) and 69; Rapho, Everts p 43; Restellini pp 52 and 53; Roger-Viollet pp 10, 11, 12, 13, 14 and 15; Schoenahl pp 49 and 50/51; Spectrum Colour Library p 61; Varig p 65.

Front cover photographs: Jean-Marc Durou and Joël Jaffre (above and below left); Spectrum Colour Library (below right).

All line drawings by Antoine Paredes, with the exception of: Clyde Surveys Limited, Maidenhead p 48.